Modern Papermaking

Techniques in Handmade Paper • 13 projects

Kelsey Pike

stashBOOKS®

an imprint of C&T Publishing

PUBLISHER: Amy Barrett-Daffin

CREATIVE DIRECTOR: Gailen Runge

SENIOR EDITOR: Roxane Cerda

EDITOR: Madison Moore

COVER/BOOK DESIGNER: April Mostek

PRODUCTION COORDINATOR: Tim Manibusan

ILLUSTRATOR: Aliza Shalit

PHOTOGRAPHY COORDINATOR: Rachel Ackley

FRONT COVER PHOTOGRAPHY by Kelsey Pike

SUBJECTS AND INSTRUCTIONAL PHOTOGRAPHY by Patricia Bordallo Dibildox; LIFESTYLE PHOTOGRAPHY by Kelsey Pike, unless otherwise noted

Published by Stash Books, an imprint of C&T Publishing, Inc., P.O. Box 1456, Lafayette, CA 94549

Library of Congress Cataloging-in-Publication Data

Names: Pike, Kelsey, author.

Title: Modern papermaking : techniques in handmade paper, 13 projects /Kelsey Pike.

Description: Lafayette, CA : Stash Books, [2023] | Includes bibliographical references and index. | Summary: "Papermaking is mesmerizing practice for a variety of visual arts fields. With a few tools and some practice, makers can craft an endless number of paper sheets. The papermaking techniques you will learn can also be used to create stand alone works of art to display, gift, and share"-- Provided by publisher.

Identifiers: LCCN 2023009985 | ISBN 9781644033074 (trade paperback) | ISBN 9781644033081 (ebook)

Subjects: LCSH: Handmade paper. | Papermaking.

Classification: LCC TS1124.5 .P55 2023 | DDC 676/.22--dc23/eng/20230302

LC record available at https://lccn.loc.gov/2023009985

Printed in China

10 9 8 7 6 5 4 3 2 1

DEDICATION

This book is dedicated to my parents, Brenda Bennett-Pike and Anthony Pike, and my husband, Tristan Wagner, whose support allowed me to study and practice this ancient and obscure craft.

ACKNOWLEDGMENTS

I'd like to thank these papermaking scholars whose work has influenced my practice: Helen Hiebert, Tim Barrett, Cathleen A. Baker, Peter & Donna Thomas.

CONTENTS

Introduction

I've spent the past 14 years studying and practicing to make the best paper I possibly can. With this book, I'm hoping to give the next generation of papermakers a head start on their journeys. I hope you fall as hopelessly in love with this craft as I have!

This book brings you into the craft with a brief history of papermaking, including how it developed over time and the science of how it works. Then the book jumps to the present day to discuss the modern tools and supplies that you'll need to make paper on your own—including lots of accessible options. I've included instructions for building some of your own papermaking tools: a mould and deckle, a couching table, and a press.

Then it's time to make your very first sheets! We'll go through the whole process from start to finish to make a simple batch of paper. The detailed instructions allow you to practice the basics. Then you'll expand your knowledge base with techniques like color and additives, shaping paper, and preparing different types of pulp. The Professional Techniques (page 68) section is for when you're ready to take your papermaking to the next level.

The final and most fun section in this book contains the projects. Here, we'll take everything you've learned to make all kinds of exciting and beautiful papers, from papers that look like the moon to a tiny envelope and card.

Papermaking is a craft that can be calming, repetitive, and meditative. Making beautiful, useful sheets from start to finish is a truly satisfying experience, sure to make you feel accomplished when you see the stack of finished papers. It can also be exciting and full of creative expression! Every project leaves ample room for fun, experimentation and your personal style. My goal is to walk you through the various parts of the process so that, in the end, you can use these techniques in your own way to make the papers of your dreams!

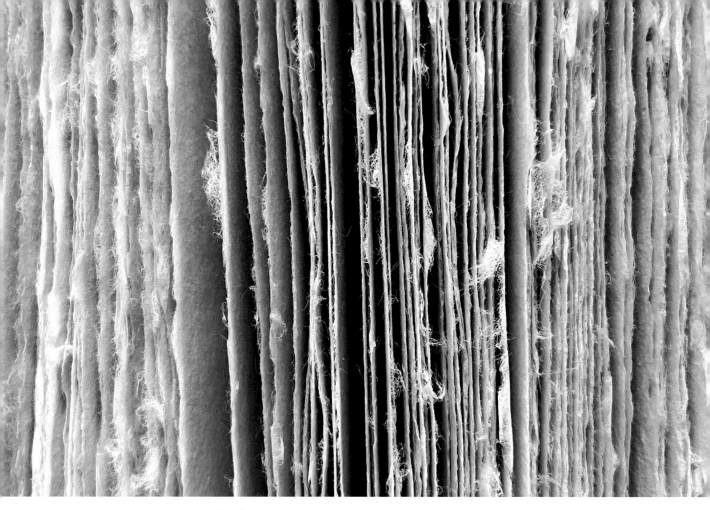

Papermaking

Paper

You probably work with paper every day, but what exactly is it? Paper is made from **cellulose pulp**. Cellulose is the main constituent of plant cell walls. Paper can be made out of any plant or anything that used to be a plant, like cotton fabric. Cellulose material becomes pulp when it is pulverized into a soft, wet mush.

Then, to form paper, the cellulose pulp is diluted by a large amount of water, and the pulp is drained through a screen.

So to make paper:

1. Beat cellulose material to a pulp

2. Dilute the pulp with water

3. Drain the water from the pulp

Before Paper

Before the invention of paper, ancient people used other materials as writing surfaces, like leaves, stones or bones, and clay tablets.

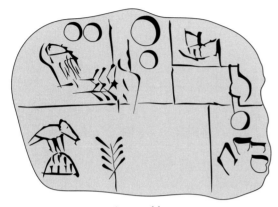

Stone tablet

About five thousand years ago, Egyptians developed papyrus. It was made by harvesting native aquatic sedge, a grass-like plant, then cutting it into thin strips. The strips were then placed in layers crosswise and pounded, which laminated them together. Papyrus was generally made in long pieces, then rolled into scrolls. It is a paper-adjacent material as it uses the same principles of creation, but it is woven in structure, not matted, and the pulp is never suspended in water.

As long as four thousand years ago, people wrote on animal skins. Parchment—made from the skins of cows, sheep, or goats—was widely used for books in Europe before the advent of paper. To form parchment, the hair is removed from the skin manually or chemically, then the surface is scraped and sanded until smooth. A particularly fine sort of parchment was called vellum, and it was made exclusively from young calves' skins. Parchment was very expensive and time-consuming to produce. Today, there are papers available called *parchment* or *vellum*, but they are instead made from plastic or wax-coated papers.

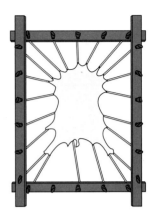

Even today, after the advent of paper, other pounded, paper-like materials—huun, amatl, amate, and tapa—are made around the world using traditional processes. These materials are made using the same principles as paper, but the pulp is never suspended in water. Tapa cloth, for instance, is made by soaking, beating, and scraping the branches of the paper mulberry tree until they are flat and smooth. The resulting material has a soft texture, much like fabric.

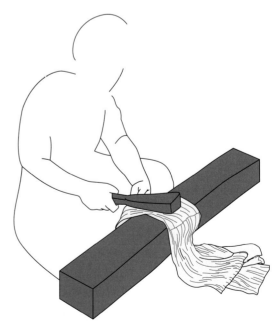

The Conception of Paper

Papermaking developed in China around two thousand years ago. It's been theorized that the technique was discovered unintentionally—women traditionally washed hemp clothes in bodies of water by pounding them with stones in tightly woven reed baskets. Beating the clothing caused bits of hemp fiber to break off and float in the water. Then, when the baskets were lifted, straining out the water, the hemp particles left in the baskets formed a very basic paper! The technology was slowly developed and then popularized by a member of the Chinese court and adviser to the emperor, Cai Lun, around 105 BCE.

This early paper was used for writing, woodblock printing by hand, and brush calligraphy. Because paper could be made from scrap materials and was cheaper to produce than the woven silk fabrics being used as writing surfaces previously, it quickly became the preferred writing surface in China. Materials like recycled fishing nets and various plant fibers were soaked, then hand beaten with mallets or rocks. The paper was then left to dry in a mould (the tool used to give shape to the paper). These earliest Chinese papermakers needed many moulds since only one piece of paper could be created at a time in each mould.

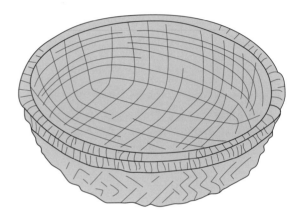

The Development of Paper

As papermaking spread, different regions modified the process to work for the types of fibers that were available in their areas and the types of paper they wanted to make (usually with qualities similar to the writing surfaces they were accustomed to), resulting in the widely varied papermaking techniques present in this chapter.

Papermaking knowledge arrived in Europe in around 1200 CE. European paper was made from worn cotton and linen rags. Rag pickers would buy people's old clothing and sell it to mills. The clothing was sorted based on color, grade, and condition. The buttons and clasps were removed, and then the rags were washed and cut into strips. Nice white rags were used to make bright white paper for manuscripts and heirloom bibles. Recycled and dirty rags and ropes were used to make disposable pamphlets and eventually paper wrappings for foods and goods. Fabrics were transformed into pulp in stamping mills, which used waterwheels or horsepower to operate giant mortar-and-pestle like devices.

Around 1680, the Hollander beater was invented, and it increased the efficiency of papermaking production. While today, industrial paper factories use other means of making pulp, the Hollander beater is still the standard for hand papermakers. This machine has a rotating wheel of blunt knives that macerates and fibrillates fibers into pulp.

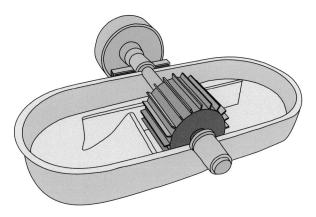

In the early American colonies, the supply of imported papers from Europe was inconsistent. So William Rittenhouse, a skilled papermaker from Holland, was recruited to immigrate to the colonies. He was the first person to make paper in North America in 1690, at his Rittenhouse Mill in Germantown, Pennsylvania. This location was perfect for papermaking because the water was clean and the town had a blacksmith who could fabricate the heavy machinery needed, a butcher who could provide sizing for the paper (see Sizing, page 12), and a weaving mill that provided scrap cotton and linen rag.

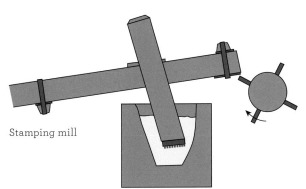

Stamping mill

All paper mills from this time period were situated near sources of water because water is necessary in every stage of the papermaking process. The first floor of these mills had stations for preparing raw materials and for forming sheets. The highest floor was the paper drying loft—filled with windows that could be used to control the humidity and air circulation to properly dry the paper.

In 1798, Nicholas Louis Robert invented a papermaking machine. The machine was hand-cranked, with an endless wire screen that rotated through the vat of pulp and water, through a press, over drying cylinders, and onto a roll. This machine replaced the need for skilled papermaking artisans. This new paper was cheaper to produce, but quality suffered. Pulp traveled through the machine in one direction only, resulting in single-direction paper grain and sheets that tore easily.

This type of machine was continually improved upon, becoming more mechanized, larger, and faster. The machines used to make all types of paper today are based on this original design. Most machines now incorporate drying cylinders at the end that are either hot, cold, or rough, causing different surface textures. Paper terminology of "hot pressed" or "cold pressed" paper is based on these cylinders.

Early fourdrinier papermaking machine

In the 1850s, it was discovered that cellulose could be extracted from wood by dissolving wood chips into pulp with strong chemicals. But these chemicals could not be thoroughly rinsed out, which made the paper acidic. This kind of paper would slowly dissolve over time, yellowing, breaking, and eventually disintegrating. Even so, mills switched over to this new technology to keep up with demand. For many years, the art of making paper by hand, with plant and fabric fibers, was all but forgotten.

Sizing

By 600 CE, paper had become so commonplace in parts of Asia that paper tea bags and toilet paper were produced. However, up until this time, all papers were made without sizing. Sizing is a substance that reduces the absorbency of paper and gives it a harder surface.

Without sizing, using watercolor paints on cotton paper is like dropping ink on a paper towel; the color bleeds and feathers. Without sizing, writing on cotton paper with a sharp pencil would tear the paper apart, as it would be too soft.

Gypsum, a soft mineral, was the first material used as sizing, followed by gelatin and starch flour. Today, papermakers use both internal sizings, meaning that they are added to the vat with the pulp, and external sizings, meaning that they are brushed onto the paper after drying.

Hand Papermaking Revival

Dard Hunter, an active member of the American Arts and Crafts movement in the 1920s, came across some old cotton papers that were made by hand and decided that papermaking knowledge had to be documented and preserved. Hunter traveled to East Asia and small islands, including Samoa, Tonga, and Fiji, where the craft was still practiced. His research became the book *Papermaking: History and Technique of an Ancient Craft*, a must-read for new papermakers. He established a mill in Connecticut for small-scale handmade paper production and established the first graduate school for paper science. It still exists today (Institute of Paper Science and Technology) in Atlanta, Georgia, and is home to the best papermaking museum in the country.

Dard Hunter
Photos provided by Robert C. Williams Museum of Papermaking at Georgia Institute of Technology

In the 1960s and 1970s, papermaking by hand enjoyed a renaissance due to the craft revival movement. Artists began experimenting with creating fine artworks with paper and pulp, not just working on finished, dry paper. Art schools and universities began offering papermaking classes. Today, there are residencies, workshops, and studios all over the world for paper artists and craftspeople.

Basic Papermaking Steps

The basic steps of papermaking are fiber preparation, pulping, pulling, couching, pressing, and drying. Each step can be completed in many ways, depending on the tools and materials at hand, and these variations can create different types of paper.

FIBER PREPARATION

First, the fiber is grown, harvested, and processed. Sometimes this process is very specialized. For example, harvesting fibers for making washi, a traditional Japanese paper made from the kozo plant, is a yearlong process. Kozo starts its life as a deciduous shrub. In the winter, after the leaves fall off, the branches are harvested, steamed, and peeled in a painstaking process. The white, inner bark is prized for making the best paper. Then, the fiber is boiled in wood ash or another caustic solution before it is finally beaten into pulp. Harvesting flax for papermaking in Europe and harvesting abaca in the Philippines are equally laborious and unique processes.

Luckily for modern papermakers, papermaking suppliers sell fibers and materials that have already been partially processed. Some steps may still be required though, like soaking, cooking, and rinsing for plant fibers. Things like cotton rags must still be sorted, washed, and shredded. Your fiber preparation will depend on your fibers.

Cooking kozo fiber

PULPING

The prepared fiber is then ground and macerated into pulp. Most modern hand papermakers use Hollander beaters or other electric appliances like blenders for pulping.

PULLING

The pulp is dispersed in a vat of water, and sheets are pulled. The tools for this vary by culture and paper type, but they are generally mesh or fabric pulled tightly over a wooden frame. In the West, the tool is called a *mould and deckle*. The method of pulling differs in different papermaking traditions. For instance, in making hanji, or traditional Korean paper, a large mould is covered with a tightly stitched bamboo screen, and then the mould is suspended by a line on one edge and dipped into the vat from side to side.

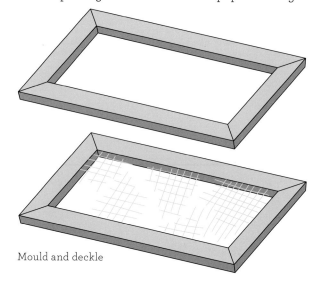

Mould and deckle

In Western-style pulling, papermakers move the mould and deckle in all directions as they remove it from the vat. This is called *the vat person's shake*. This motion mats the fibers together, producing strong bonds in every direction. This motion takes years of practice to perfect, and every papermaker has a unique shake.

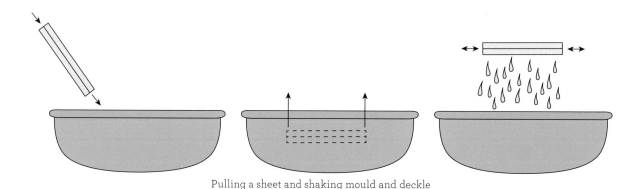

Pulling a sheet and shaking mould and deckle

TIP

Paper sheets can be poured instead of pulled. See Using a Deckle Box (page 67).

COUCHING

The pulp, now a wet sheet, is then transferred to a pile of wet sheets—a post—from the mould and deckle. This transfer is called *couching*. In Europe, sheets were traditionally couched with wet wool felt between each sheet. When making hanji, the sheets are laid on top of each other for pressing with only a single thread placed between them. Later, the thread is delicately pulled to separate the sheets. In some traditions, paper is dried on the screen without couching or pressing. Modern papermakers generally use polyester interfacing between the sheets and might also employ a curved couching table, which allows each sheet to detach from the mould more cleanly and with less pressure. The interfacing sheets are called *felts*, even though they are often made from another material.

Hanji couching

PRESSING

After the sheets are all in the post, they are pressed. Pressing removes water, and the pressure aids in fiber cohesion. Any system that places the papers under adequate pressure will work. Traditionally, large wooden screw presses were used, and today most papermakers use hydraulic presses.

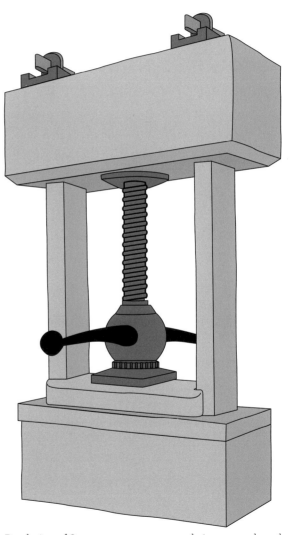

Rendering of Sampson paper press, made in 1790 and used at Wookey Hole Mill in England. Currently housed at Robert C. Williams Museum of Papermaking at Georgia Institute of Technology.

DRYING

The final step in papermaking is drying. The drying process has a tremendous effect on the surface texture of the finished paper. In some traditions, the papers are brushed onto flat surfaces, such as heated boards. This creates papers with a smooth surface on one side and a rougher surface on the other. In other cases, the papers are hung to dry on the felts, or several sheets are pressed together and hung (these groups are called *spurs*). Some papermaking studios today employ dry boxes that use fans and absorbent cotton blotting paper (also called *blotters*).

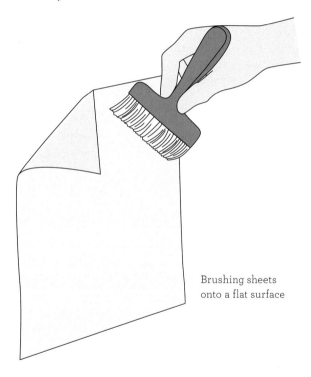

Brushing sheets onto a flat surface

The Science of Paper

Cellulose fibers can form the strong bonds that make paper because of an interaction that takes place between water and cellulose. Water molecules have negative and positive poles and attract each other, forming hydrogen bonds. Cellulose fibers are made of long chains of cellulose molecules. Parts of the cellulose chains, called *hydroxyl groups*, stick up. A water molecule can bond with a hydroxyl group as easily as with another water molecule.

Beating fibers splits them into small, slender strands called *fibrils*. This allows more hydroxyl groups to be created, allowing more water to bond with the fiber. The more fiber is beaten, the more water attaches and the longer it takes for water to drain from the paper. As the paper dries, hydrogen bonds hold the paper together, actually pulling the fibrils tighter and closer together. Because of this, pulp that is beaten longer will shrink in size as it dries.

Plant fibers are made of a variety of compounds, not just cellulose. The main components are cellulose, hemicellulose, and lignin. Cellulose's defining characteristic is that it absorbs

The random way that cellulose fibers lock together, creating a matted surface and giving the defining paper texture

Photo provided by Robert C. Williams Museum of Papermaking at Georgia Institute of Technology

water and swells. Hemicellulose increases the flexibility of cellulose. Lignin acts as a natural binder and support in woody plants. Lignin cannot absorb water and is therefore removed from plant fibers through a chemical process before papermaking.

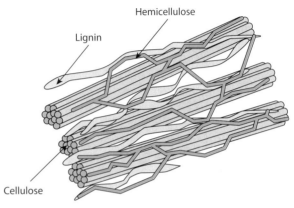

All plants also contain various other extracts such as minerals, proteins, fatty acids, resinous acids, and phenols. These variations result in each plant fiber's having unique color, scent, and other physical properties.

Tools and Supplies

Setting Up a Small Studio Space

There are many kinds of spaces that will work for making paper. When choosing yours, consider two important characteristics:

- Flooring that won't be damaged by water, ideally with a drain

- A convenient source of water for filling buckets and vats—hoses are ideal, but you can fill up at a sink

A garage or a basement with a utility sink could make a great papermaking studio. Weather permitting, you could set up an outdoor area near a garden hose. In a pinch, a large bathroom with a walk-in shower can even work! If none of these are options, you may be able to get away with a thorough mopping and drying of a less ideal space (like your kitchen) after each papermaking session.

In addition to the wet papermaking area, it can be nice to have a separate dry area to store materials and work with finished sheets. Having a separate space can prevent accidentally splashing water over your beautiful stack of dry paper!

My papermaking studio on the mezzanine at the Cherry Pit Collective in Kansas City

Tools

MOULD AND DECKLE

The mould and deckle is the papermaker's primary tool. It's a two-part tool made up of a screen (mould) and a frame (deckle) that is used to collect the paper pulp for each sheet. The size of the set determines the size of the finished paper. Moulds are not mass manufactured, so buying one can be pricey. I recommend building one yourself to start, until you're ready to invest in a beautiful mould and deckle handmade by a skilled craftsperson. These sets are referred to by the approximate size of paper they produce (some fibers create a wider deckle edge, while others will shrink while drying); expect up to ½˝ (1.2cm) variance in actual paper size. See Build a Basic Mould and Deckle (page 32) to DIY your own. You can also purchase multi-sheet deckles that allow you to make more than one piece of paper at a time.

NOTE

Did you know the beautiful, uneven edges of handmade paper are called *deckled edges*, after the tool that makes them? These edges are created when small amounts of pulp creep under the edge of the deckle during pulling. In the past, they would have been cut off, but today they are celebrated as a sign of hand-manufacturing!

To care for a mould, clean away all pulp while it's wet, then dry the mould and store it level and horizontal. Storing the mould upright or hanging it can cause warping that will make it harder to use in the future.

VAT

A vat is a container used to hold the pulp and water mixture (called a *slurry*). Traditionally, vats were made of wood or metal, but today, plastic is most commonly used for ease of cleanup. Choose a tub with a top opening at least a hand's width larger than your largest mould on all sides, and at least 6˝ (15cm) deep. The larger the vat, the easier it will be to make sheets that are a consistent thickness. Concrete mixing tubs are popular options, but also look in the storage tub section. Restaurant supply stores often have large tubs. My favorite vat is made for hydroponics and has a handy lid.

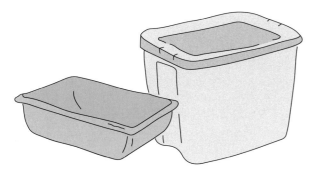

FELTS

The piece of material that separates sheets from one another is called a *felt* because traditionally, papermakers used wool felts. Now, regardless of the actual material, this tool is called a felt. Today, wool felt can be expensive and stinky, so I recommend using polyester interfacing to separate sheets.

In a pinch, wool materials, like old blankets, can be cut to size and used as felts. Cotton fabric, such as an old bedsheet, could also work if necessary, but the paper will tend to stick to cellulose material. Note: Don't even try to use those tiny sheets of synthetic craft felt! They're not made of wool and don't work well for this.

Interfacing

Any brand or type of nonfusible interfacing will work, but I recommend 65 Pellon Stabilizer, which is very heavyweight and 70% polyester. Buy it by the bolt at a craft store, and cut it to the size you need. Thinner interfacings can cause wrinkling in the paper as it dries. All interfacings come with a surface protectant, so before using them for the first time, soak, rinse, and dry the interfacing.

TOWELS

Interfacing works great to separate the sheets, but because it's a synthetic material, it doesn't absorb any water itself. So you must use something absorbent at the bottom and top of the post in order to press the sheets properly. I like to use old bath towels cut to size. A nearby basket of towels will also be helpful for spills.

PRESSBOARDS

Pressboards are sturdy boards used for transporting and pressing wet sheets. Choose any material that can withstand repeated soakings with water, high pressure, and that will be sturdy enough to support the weight of the post as it is moved around. Hardwood sealed with spar varnish or polyurethane is a classic and accessible choice. Acrylic or plastic sheets are a good choice for resistance to mold and mildew. It's best to buy these materials in large sheets and ask a home store employee or a friend with a table saw to cut them to size.

PRESS

A press applies pressure to the post to remove water and aid in fiber cohesion. Professional papermaking studios use hydraulic presses. I use one with a ten-ton jack. Other kinds, like book presses or flower presses, will apply less pressure but will still work well to get you started.

Book press

The press needs to apply pressure evenly across the surface of the pressboards and apply it slowly, increasing over time. Once maximum pressure is reached, leave the post for at least 10-20 minutes. See Build a Basic Press (page 36) to make your own press.

Hydraulic press

Other Options

If you don't have access to any kind of press, you can use other means to apply pressure to the wet sheets.

Put the post on the ground with one pressboard underneath and another on top. Then add at least 100 pounds (45kg) to the top. Add weight by:

- Putting two 5-gallon buckets on top of the stack and then slowly filling them with water, alternating buckets to keep them balanced.

- Slowly stacking plate weights or dumbbells on the stack.

- Standing on the stack! Slowly add your weight, and be careful not to slip; it's usually best to have a friend nearby to steady you.

DRYING

After pressing, it's time to let the paper dry. How you dry the paper will decide its surface texture.

Hang Drying

Leave the paper on the felt, and hang the sheets on a line with a clothespin to dry. With a fan in front of the line, they will usually dry overnight. If this is the drying plan you're using, separate the post at regular intervals (about every five sheets) with a towel when you're pulling so that you're not trying to pin up a heavy mass of paper later. I always recommend leaving at least two sheets together, as a single sheet tends to curl as it dries. Hang drying is my preferred drying method for most sheets.

Dry Box

A dry box is a stack of alternating absorbent material and corrugated cardboard, with a fan on one side and a weight on top. Blotting paper (sheets of absorbent cotton paper with no sizing, available at art supply stores) and cotton linters are great options for absorbent materials. Cotton linters are usually shipped folded, so if you're using them for a dry box, make sure you specifically ask that they be shipped flat.

After you press the sheets, peel them off the felts, and place them in a single layer on top of a sheet of absorbent material; then place another sheet of the absorbent material on top. Place a sheet of corrugated cardboard above and below each paper sandwich, and repeat until all the wet paper is in the dry box. Top with a weight, and turn on the fan. Anywhere between 50 and 200 pounds (22.6 and 90.7 KG) of pressure will work.

The absorbent material and cardboard absorb the water from the paper, then the airflow from the fan carries the moisture away. The weight ensures that the sheets don't curl as they dry. This method takes up less space than hanging, but it means that you have to handle the wet sheets without their felts, which can be tricky to do without damaging them.

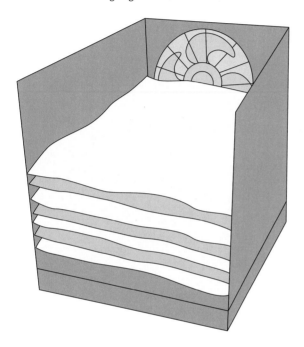

Rolling Flat

Another option is to affix the sheets to a flat surface to dry. Peel the wet sheet from the felt, press it onto a clean window, then use a rolling pin, sponge, or your fingertips to affix it to the glass, especially around the edges. A variety of smooth surfaces, like sheets of melamine, laminate board, or acrylic sheeting can be used instead of a window. This method gives the two sides of the sheet different textures, as the side against the flat surface will take on that smooth texture. After the sheet is completely dry, remove it from the drying surface.

Heat Drying

Paper can be dried quickly with heat, which can be great when making samples but is often less convenient for large batches. When using heat drying, start by pressing the paper as usual to remove most of the water. All heat methods create steam as the water in the sheet boils and evaporates, so use caution not to burn your skin.

One accessible option is to use a clothes iron. Place the sheet on a heat-safe surface (such as an ironing board), then place a dry towel on top of the wet sheet. Turn the iron to the hottest setting, then slowly run the iron across the surface of the towel until the paper is dry. Another option is to roll the wet sheet onto glass, then use a heat gun or hair dryer to blow hot air onto the surface of the paper until it is dry. The method I like best is to use an electric warming tray. Simply plop the wet sheet onto the glass surface of the tray and turn it on until the sheet is dry.

COUCHING TABLE

A couching table is a curved surface to couch paper on top of. The curve helps the paper to release from the mould with less pressure. It'll save you a ton of headaches and air bubbles! See Build a Couching Table (page 34) to make one. In a pinch, several towels can be folded to create a curved surface instead.

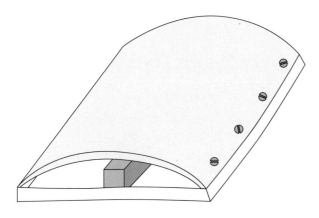

TABLE

You need a main work table. A plastic folding table with adjustable leg heights is great if you're buying something new.

BUCKETS AND CONTAINERS

Paper studios need a wide assortment of buckets and containers for pulp and water. I like to use 5-gallon hardware store buckets with handles because they're sturdy, they're easy to clean, they're not too heavy to carry, and they stack easily. Smaller containers are great for scooping pulp and for preparing additives and pigments. I like to use a 4-cup measuring cup with a handle for quick and easy measuring and pouring. No need to buy something new if you've got some containers lying around!

STRAINERS

A fine mesh strainer will come in handy for cleaning. When emptying the vat, use a strainer to separate pulp from water, even if the vat seems empty of pulp, to prevent clogged drains. If there's a substantial amount of pulp left, bag it and save it in the refrigerator for later.

SCALE

A scale is necessary to weigh various materials before pulping. Get one that goes up to a pound (0.45kg) but also has finer increments in ounces or grams. Digital and analog scales both work well. I use a decommissioned postage scale.

MISCELLANEOUS

To use papermaking additives, you need a selection of measuring cups and spoons that are no longer used for food. You also need a roll of high-quality duct tape and permanent markers for various projects. Finally, I call for EVA foam sheeting for several projects.

Pulping Tools

There are thousands of kinds of paper in the world—soft and fluffy toilet paper, sturdy cardboard, translucent lamp shades, absorbent tea bags, waterproof glassine, and everything in between. Every characteristic of paper can be fine-tuned through preparation in the beater. As a beginner in the world of hand papermaking, consider how a paper will be used when choosing your materials and techniques. Of course, if your goal is to have some fun experimenting and making paper, you're ready to go!

HOLLANDER-BEATEN PULP

Like I mentioned, pulp prepared in a Hollander beater is the crème de la crème for hand papermaking. The mechanical beating action of the Hollander beater creates many fibrils on the fibers, forming cellulose bonds that are long and strong. Hollander beaters can fine-tune pulp to create many kinds of paper, from fluffy to crispy. No need to order a Hollander beater right away though—there are many options to access this kind of pulp.

Ordering Pulp Online

You can order beaten pulp from papermaking suppliers online. They will process the pulp in their large beaters to the exact specifications of the order, including fiber content, beating time, and additives. After beating, they drain the pulp, seal it in a bucket, and mail it right to you. The pulp is perishable, so use it within a few days of receiving it, or refrigerate it.

This Hollander beater is a "Critter Beater" made by Mark Lander in New Zealand. I've named this particular beater in my studio Hollis.

Ordering from a Local Papermaker

Similarly, many papermakers and paper studios beat pulp to order for people in their areas. For instance, I'll beat pulp at my studio for anyone willing to pick it up. To find someone in your area, try searching "papermaking" and your city.

Renting a Hollander Beater

You may be lucky enough to live in an area with a community paper studio! If that's the case, you can usually rent time on a Hollander beater after you've taken introductory classes. Also ask if this is possible at local colleges with papermaking programs. To learn more about using one, see Using a Hollander Beater (page 77).

USING A BLENDER FOR PULP

When you're just starting out, a blender is a great option for making your own pulp. The chopping action of a blender will make any fiber shorter. It doesn't make the same number of hydrogen bonding sites that pounding or beating does, but it's perfectly fine for recycled papers. Any blender used for papermaking needs to be reserved for crafts only and should not be used for food preparation. Note: Even if you have a Hollander beater, you'll still need a blender to prepare papermaking additives (see Using Papermaking Additives, page 52).

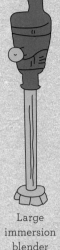

STAND BLENDER OR IMMERSION BLENDER?

Stand blenders are inexpensive and easy to pick up at thrift stores. Choose one with a blade that comes off for easy cleaning. But if you plan to make a lot of pulp and don't want to be limited by the size of the stand container, try an immersion blender. Immersion blenders can blend pulp in larger bowls or buckets. If you're ready to invest a bit more, a commercial-grade immersion blender with a 18″–20″ (45.7–50.8cm) shaft from a restaurant supplier can blend an entire 5-gallon bucket in a few seconds.

Large immersion blender

HAND BEATING

Fibers can be beaten by hand using a mallet or bat. The beating action opens the fibers to form fibrils, but the process can be labor intensive and slow. To try it out, squeeze the water out of a handful of fiber; place it on a wooden cutting board or other sturdy, clean surface; and hammer away! When the fibers form a thin layer over the surface, scrape them into a ball and beat again. Repeat this process until the fibers form a homogeneous pulp when dispersed in water, then continue with another handful of pulp. Try it out with freshly cooked kozo pulp for best results.

OTHER DIY OPTIONS

A lot of household devices that are used to grind or stir can be rigged into pulp-processing machines. A food processor can be used in the same manner as a blender. I've also seen ingenious contraptions that were repurposed from sink garbage disposals to make pulp. Another option is a drill with a paint-mixing attachment, which can provide enough beating for some fibers. This can be a handy tool to have around the studio for mixing additives into pulp. Research some of these ideas online if you want to use more unconventional pulping methods.

Common Sheet pulps

Pulps

SHEET PULPS

These pulps are preprocessed fibers available from papermaking suppliers; they are available in large sheets and sold by dry weight. Most of the work has already been done for you! In general, all of these pulps in sheet form can easily be blended using the same techniques as those used for recycled paper (see Recycling Paper, page 30).

Cotton Sheet Pulp

Cotton is a bright white, short fiber that lends bulk and fluffiness to paper. It has the highest percentage of cellulose content of any plant and is therefore a perfect choice for papermaking. There are two common types of cotton readily available from papermaking suppliers:

Cotton on the stem

- **Linter:** Linter is the shortest of the cotton fibers that grows next to the seed and is too short for spinning into thread for weaving or knitting.

- **Rag Half Stuff:** Rag half stuff, also called *comber noil*, is a slightly longer cotton fiber that is a by-product of the spinning process.

Abaca Sheet Pulp

Abaca plant

Abaca fiber is a long fiber harvested from a herbaceous plant native to the Philippines and often used to make rope. It is naturally a light tan color but is also available in a more processed, sun-"bleached" variation that is creamy white. Paper made from abaca has good wet strength, fold endurance, and surface hardness, making it a perfect choice for paper used for art media including watercolor, bookbinding, and drawing.

Other Sheet Pulps

You may find other sheet pulps available from papermaking suppliers, such as flax, bamboo, esparto, jute, sisal, and hemp. Learn about the specifics by reading manufacturer instructions and researching. Check out Resources (page 124) for more places to look.

PLANT FIBERS

Bark Fibers

Kozo, gampi, and mitsumata are bark fibers traditionally used to make paper in Asian regions. They are extremely long and strong fibers that can make translucent, thin, flexible paper that is still extremely durable. They require cooking before beating, though sometimes these fibers are available precooked and still wet from suppliers (see Cooking Plant Fibers, page 50). In either case, hand beating tends to work well for these fibers. Processing in a blender is not recommended.

Bundle of Kozo fiber

Other Plant Fibers

Many other plant materials can be made into paper, including many things growing in your yard or garden, but each will require specific processing that may include drying, steaming, retting, scraping, or cooking. Check out Cooking Plant Fibers (page 50) to learn more about fiber cooking.

FABRICS

With a Hollander beater, fabrics can be transformed into pulp for papermaking. Choose fabrics that are 100% cellulose like cotton, linen, hemp, silk, or blends of these fibers. Fabrics with any percentage of synthetic fibers are unsuitable for papermaking.

Scraps from sewing and quilting, worn clothing or bedding, and new fabric yardage can all be used. To prepare fabric for beating, wash it in a washing machine once with detergent and then again with no additives. Remove any buttons, elastic, or areas of uncertain fiber content. Then cut the fabric into ¼″–1″ (6mm–2.5cm) pieces and add them to the Hollander beater. A rotary cutter and cutting mat work well for chopping up the fabric.

WOVEN OR KNIT FABRIC?

Because of the mechanical action of the Hollander beater, woven fabrics are much easier to process than are knit fabrics. Woven fabrics are usually used for bed sheets, jeans, and button-down shirts. Generally, fabric with no stretch is woven. Knit fabrics are usually found in T-shirts, sweatpants, and other stretchy garments. If a knit fabric must be processed into pulp, cut it into the smallest pieces possible before beating it.

RECYCLING PAPER

Making new paper from waste paper can be a great exercise in recycling that produces beautiful and usable paper! The key is selecting the right raw materials. Many paper products in our daily lives are made from recycled paper. Each time paper is recycled, the fibers become shorter and weaker. Most commercial papers are made from short, chemically processed wood fibers. For instance, fine writing or printing paper is recycled into cereal boxes or newspapers, then into corrugated cardboard, egg cartons, or toilet paper.

I don't recommend making pulp from items lower down in this cycle. The fibers are extremely short and will make paper that is brittle and weak. Similarly, each time the pulp is commercially processed for recycling, more additives and chemicals are added. These additives make the end result of the papers uncertain and can also make the vat unpleasant or dangerous to have your hands in! For the same reasons, I also advise against recycling any paper with a glossy coating, like magazine paper or photo paper.

Items that come early in the cycle are a good bet for recycling into new paper—office paper, printer paper, writing paper, art papers (except cheap kids' construction paper), envelopes, and mail.

Recycling Papers with Cotton Content

Cotton printmaking paper scraps are superior options for recycling into new paper—see if a letterpress print shop in your area might want to donate cutoffs! Fine art and watercolor papers with cotton content work wonderfully too. If you've got a sturdy enough blender, 100% cotton matte board for framing also makes beautiful papers.

MIXING PULPS

Beautiful and functional recycled paper can be made by mixing recycled scraps with cotton or abaca pulp. Add a pinch of these known fibers to recycled papers before blending, or blend the two pulps separately and mix after.

BLENDING PULP

With any paper you plan to recycle, start by removing any noncellulose bits like plastic windows, gummed edges, and staples. Then use a paper shredder or scissors to cut the paper into small pieces.

Add the scraps to a bucket, and soak in hot water overnight. The next day, strain the water off. Add water to the blender, then add the wet paper. Start on a low blender setting for 1–2 seconds at a time, then use a higher blending setting as the mixture begins to spin. If the pulp is not moving well, stop the blender and stir with a spoon or spatula.

If paper is bound up in the blades, always unplug the blender before reaching inside. If the motor of the blender begins to smell or smoke, stop it right away, and give it a break.

Deciding when the pulp is ready to go is up to you! If you like it chunky, with bits of the paper's old life visible, a few seconds might do it. If you want a smooth, homogeneous mixture, blend for longer. Take it slow, not blending more than about 10–20 seconds at a time.

BUILD A BASIC MOULD AND DECKLE

MATERIALS

- Canvas stretcher bars

    Four 13″ (33cm) pieces

    Four 11″ (28cm) pieces
- Staple gun and ⅜″ (9mm) staples (stainless steel preferred)
- Two-part epoxy glue (5-minute set time)
- Spar exterior varnish
- 1 linear foot of polypropylene screening mesh
- Mallet or hammer
- Scrub brush and powder cleaner
- Permanent marker
- Hairdryer

Notes about Materials

The dimensions listed for the frame will make a sheet of paper about 8″ × 10″ (20 × 25cm), depending on the thickness of the bars. This size mould and deckle will work for all of the projects listed in this book. Canvas stretcher bars are available from art supply stores or from online art supply retailers.

Polypropylene screen mesh is available from Carriage House Paper. All other supplies are available at hardware stores. The hair dryer does not need to be used exclusively for crafts, but a cheap one will work fine if you're buying new. Cleaning powders like Bon Ami, Comet, or Bar Keepers Friend are great options.

Build the Frames

1. Assemble the stretcher bars into two empty frames, using a mallet to hammer the bars together.

2. Apply two-part epoxy to the corner joints, let it set, and then staple across the seam to hold the pieces secure.

3. If you intend to use the mould and deckle on a regular basis, it needs to be coated against water damage. Coat the wood surface of each frame with a layer or two of spar varnish. Once dry, set aside one frame—this is the complete deckle.

Attach the Mesh to the Mould

1. Place the remaining frame onto the mesh, and trace around the outside with permanent marker. Cut the mesh to this size.

2. Staple the mesh onto the flattest, smoothest side of the frame with the staple gun, aligning the staples at a 45° angle to the frame. **Ⓐ**

3. After the screen is securely attached, use epoxy to coat the edges of the screen and cover the staples. Let it set.

Preparing for Use

1. Remove the coating from the polypropylene screen by soaking the mould in water for a few minutes, then scrub the surface of the mesh in all directions with a scrub brush and powder cleaner. Rinse well, and allow to dry.

2. If the mesh is loose at all, tighten it by blowing warm air across the screen with a few smooth strokes of a hairdryer. Work in circles from one end to another until it becomes taut.

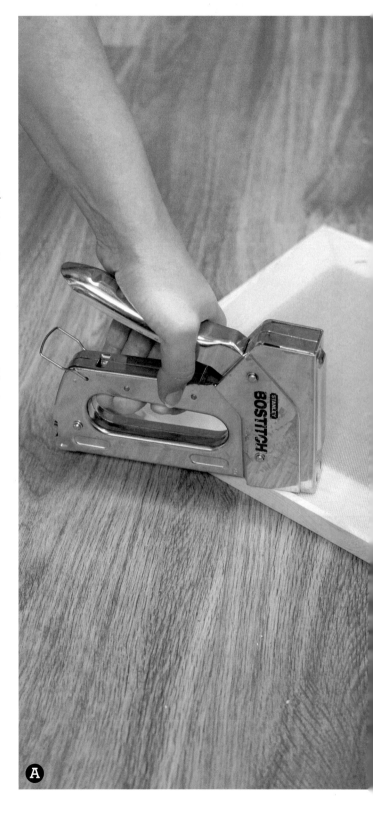

BUILD A COUCHING TABLE

MATERIALS

- ¾″ (19mm)-thick plywood pressboard coated in exterior spar varnish, cut to 16″ × 18″ (40 × 46cm)
- 1″ thick × 2″ wide (2.5 × 5cm) lumber, cut to 18″ (46cm) long
- Drill
- Stainless steel wood trim screws:

    Three 2½″ (6.4cm) screws

    Eight ⅝″ (1.6cm) screws
- ⅛″ (3mm)-thick high-density polyethylene (HDPE) or flexible plastic, cut to 17″ × 18″ (43 × 46cm)

Notes about Materials

All materials are available from hardware stores.

Construct

1. Place the lumber in the center of the pressboard, with the narrowest side down. Attach to the pressboard using three evenly spaced 2½˝ (6.4cm) screws.

2. Attach the flexible plastic to one side of the pressboard with four ⅝˝ (1.6cm) screws. Space the screws evenly across the plastic edge.

3. Carefully bend the flexible plastic to the other side of the pressboard, and attach with another four ⅝˝ (1.6cm) screws. **Ⓐ Ⓑ**

Ⓐ

Ⓑ

BUILD A BASIC PRESS

MATERIALS

- 4 pieces 2˝ × 4˝ (5 × 10cm) lumber, cut into four 22˝ (56cm) lengths
- 4 galvanized or stainless steel threaded rods, 12˝ (25cm) long, ⁵/₁₆˝ (8mm) diameter
- Four ⁵/₁₆˝ (8mm) galvanized or stainless steel wing nuts
- Eight ⁵/₁₆˝ (8mm) galvanized or stainless steel washers
- Four ⁵/₁₆˝ (8mm) galvanized or stainless steel locking nuts
- Drill with ⅜˝ (9.5mm) drill bit
- Two ¾˝ (19mm)-thick, 16˝ × 18˝ (40 × 46cm) plywood pressboards, coated in exterior spar varnish

Notes about Materials

All materials are available from hardware stores. This basic press will provide adequate pressure for papermaking while being easy to build and store. It works in conjunction with two pressboards.

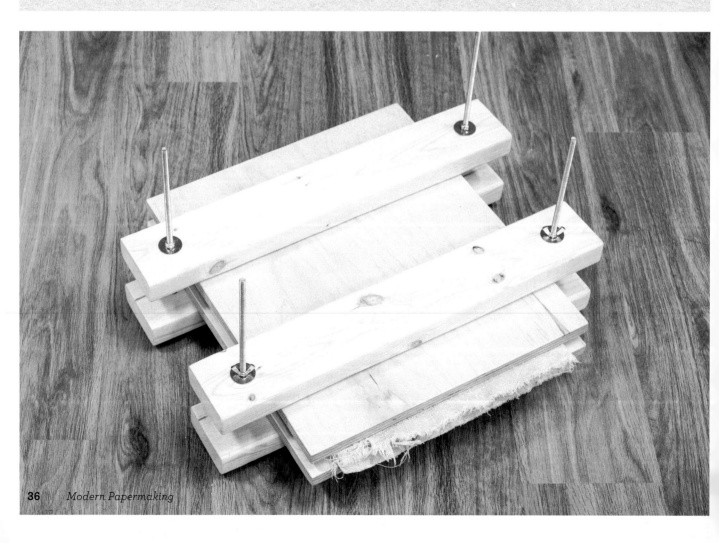

Construct

1. Drill a hole in each short end of all pieces of lumber 2″ (5cm) from the edge, centered. These pieces are the pressing apparatuses. **Ⓐ**

Assemble

When you're ready to use the press, assemble following these directions. Otherwise, store the parts unassembled. Disassemble the parts after use for easy storage.

1. Take two of the pressing apparatuses, and set the other two aside for now. Screw a locking nut, then a washer, onto each threaded rod. Place the four rods through the holes on the two pressing apparatuses, then set on the floor or table with the rod sticking up. The nut and washer should be below the wood.

2. Place the two boards about 6″ (15cm) apart. **Ⓑ**

3. Place a paper post on the pressboard. Then place the pressboard on the pressing apparatuses, on top of the two pieces of wood and between the rods. Top the stack with the second pressboard. **Ⓒ**

4. Thread the other two pressing apparatuses onto the rods. Screw a washer and then a wing nut onto each rod, securing the apparatuses.

5. Slowly tighten the wing nuts to apply pressure to the post. Apply as much pressure as possible manually. **Ⓓ**

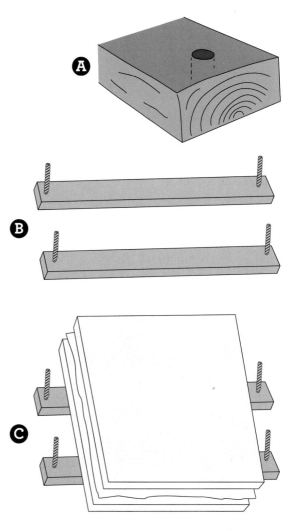

MAKE BASIC SHEETS

Before we start to explore the large variety of techniques that can be used in papermaking, we're going to make a basic batch to experience the complete process in the simplest way possible. This recipe will make 15 to 20 sheets of paper.

MATERIALS

- Recycled paper scraps 6 oz (160g)
- Stand blender
- Mould and deckle around 8″ × 10″ (20 × 25cm)
- Felts (interfacing suggested)
- Towels
- Bucket (5 gallon)
- Mesh strainer
- Vat
- Clothespins
- Clothesline
- Fan

Make Pulp with a Blender

For this simple first sheet, we're going to recycle existing scrap paper into pulp. For more on recycled paper pulp, see Recycling Paper (page 30).

1. Gather and sort paper scraps to recycle into pulp. Remove any staples and plastic windows. Use a paper shredder or hand tear the paper into pieces small enough to easily fit in the blender. Toss the scraps into a bucket, and fill with enough hot water to cover them completely. Soak overnight.

2. The next morning, pour the water and paper through a mesh strainer. This will remove any ink or other particulates that have seeped into the water. **A**

3. Fill the stand blender ¾ of the way full of water, then add a handful of wet paper scraps from the strainer. Put on the blender lid, and plug the blender in. **B** **C**

4. Start the blender on a pulse setting. Blend for a second or two at a time until the paper scraps become chopped and move freely. Then use a higher setting and blend for up to 10 seconds at a time. If at any time the pulp stops moving, stop the blender and add more water. If you suspect paper scraps are tangled around the blender blades, remove the blender cup from the stand or unplug it before taking the top off and reaching your hands inside to untangle the scraps. If the blender has no trouble blending the amount of pulp you add, try adding less water and more pulp in future batches until you find just the right recipe for your blender.

A

B

C

5. Continue blending until the mixture becomes one homogeneous color. For subsequent batches, you can choose to keep the pulp chunky if you like the look, but for this first sheet, blend it evenly.

6. Repeat Steps 3–5 until all the paper is blended.

NOTE: SIZING

Most commercial papers already contain sizing, so it is not always necessary to add more. Remember that sizing reduces the absorbency of paper and hardens it, making it possible to paint or write on it without bleeding or tearing. To determine whether your batch needs sizing, I recommend drying a pulp sample and testing it out with different media and techniques. If your paper needs sizing, it would be added at this stage, after the pulp is prepared. Since this batch is your first test anyway, proceed without adding sizing. For more information, see Sizing (page 56).

Fill the Vat

1. Fill the vat with at least 5˝ (13cm) of slurry. The amount of pulp and water needed to do this will depend on the size of your vat, but this is the minimum depth to comfortably fit your mould. As a general rule, for every 10 parts water, add 1 part prepared pulp. Stir well!

Pull Sheet

1. Before pulling each sheet, stir the vat to make sure the pulp is suspended in the water and not sunk to the bottom of the vat. Stack the deckle on top of the mould.

2. Hold the mould and deckle with straight arms, perpendicular to the vat surface. In a smooth motion, scoop the mould down and into the vat at a 45° angle.

3. As soon as the mould and deckle is submerged, rotate it to be parallel to the surface of the water, and bring it straight up and out of the slurry. When the surface of the mould reaches the surface of the water, surface tension will make the mould feel very heavy, but use more force to quickly overcome this pressure.
B

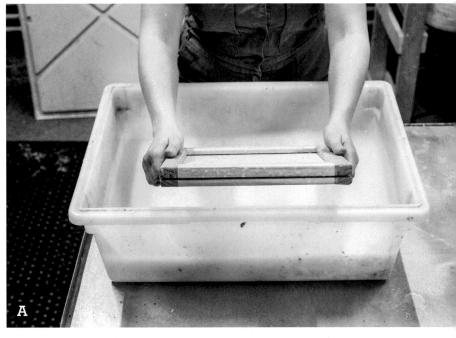

A

B

4. As soon as the mould and deckle is above the surface of the water, start your vat person's shake. Each person's shake is unique, and over time you'll develop your own style. To start, try a small shake away from your body and then toward your body, then three small rocking motions from left to right. The goal is to spread the fibers evenly across the surface of the mould and knit them closely together. As you shake, the water will drain from the mould. In the beginning, the surface will appear glassy, as it is primarily water. As soon as the surface of the mould starts to look like oatmeal rather than glass, stop shaking. **C**-**E**

5. Hold the mould perfectly level over the vat as water continues to drain away. When the water slows to a trickle, tilt the mould so water can continue to pour out of one corner. If the pulp moves at all, you've tilted too early—allow it to drain longer next time.

6. When the water stream slows to single drops, the sheet is ready to be couched. **F**

7. Set the mould and deckle down. Remove the deckle, being careful not to let water from the frame drip onto the surface of the paper.

8. As you continue, add a bit more pulp to the water after every sheet or two.

NOTE: KISSING OFF

If something goes wrong with a sheet and you'd rather not save it, simply turn the mould upside down on the surface of the water in the vat. The pulp will drop back in, and you can reuse it. This is called *kissing off*. Stir well before continuing.

Couch Sheet

1. Prepare a couching area. You can do so by folding a few towels into a mound, then adding a flat towel on top to make the mound smooth. If you've already built a couching table, simply top it with a wet towel or two.

2. Top the couching area with a clean, premoistened felt (a.k.a. polyester interfacing). You'll need wet felts all through the couching process, so either keep a stack nearby in a water tub or wet the felts one by one as needed. The felts must be thoroughly wet to grab the paper.

3. Align the long edge of the mould along one edge of the felt, holding the mould on its side, perpendicular to the table. Grasp one long edge of the mould with each hand.

4. The transfer of the sheet from mould to felt should be in one smooth rocking motion. Press the mould down to come in contact with the felt, transferring pressure from one hand to the other. Apply pressure to the frame, transferring the sheet from the mould to the felt. **A**-**F**

NOTE: TROUBLESHOOTING
If the pulp sticks to the mould, apply more pressure throughout the motion next time. If the sheet appears splattered, or the edges run off, allow the sheet to drain longer and/or couch more slowly.

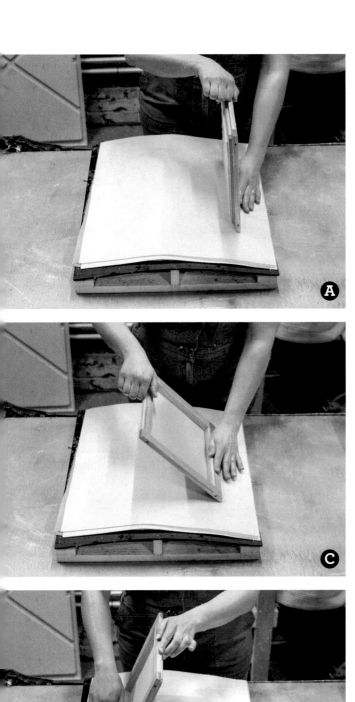

Build a Post

1. After pulling and couching the first sheet, simply repeat the papermaking process until all the pulp is used or until you have the desired number of sheets. After each sheet is couched, top it with another clean, wet felt, then couch another sheet directly on top of it.

2. The sheets will pile into a mound shape. Try to align each sheet, couching in approximately the same place on the felt. If the sheets are significantly misaligned, the mismatched sheet shapes might emboss onto each other when they are pressed. **Ⓐ**

3. Every 5 sheets or so, top the wet felt with a moist towel. Then, add another wet felt and continue couching on top. This towel will act as a buffer so that any imperfections in the sheets or alignment aren't transferred to the whole post. This also allows you to easily separate the post into sections for drying.

4. After about 10 sheets (two stacks of 5 separated by a towel), move the post to the pressing area. If you're using towels under the post, lift the post by the flat towel onto a pressboard, leaving the folded towels behind. If you're using a couching table, pull the post from the rounded table onto a pressboard. **Ⓑ**

> ### NOTE: POST SIZES
> Anytime you change paper sizes, you need to start a new post. Each sheet in a post should be the same size and in the same position on the felts.

Ⓐ

Ⓑ

Press

1. Press the post using any of the methods described in Press (page 22). Optional: After pressing once, sort through the post and remove the wet towels, replacing them with dry towels, and then press again. This will remove more water and allow the sheets to dry more quickly.

Clean Up

While the press is working, clean up the studio!

1. First, empty the vat. Pour cupfuls of slurry into a strainer. This can be done over a bucket or over a sink drain. Allow the pulp to drain in the strainer, then work into a ball and press to remove more water. If you like, you can store this leftover pulp in a baggie in the fridge to use at a later time, or you can let it dry and toss it in a recycling bin. **A** **B**

2. Clean all pulp surfaces. Clean all pulp off the mould and deckle, making sure to spray water through the mesh from the back of the mould to prevent small fibers from drying and clogging the screen. Wipe down the vat with a sponge, and rinse. Rinse or wipe any other pulp-covered surfaces, like the table or floor. Pulp is always so much easier to clean while wet! If allowed to dry, it will have to be painstakingly peeled and scraped. **C**

3. Allow all supplies to dry thoroughly before storing them. Wipe everything down with a dry cloth, or allow to dry for a few hours with a fan. Store mould and deckles flat, not upright or hanging, to prevent warping.

A

B

C

Hang Dry

1. After the pressing time for your chosen method is complete, remove the pressure. Remove the pressed-together bundles of interfacing with paper sheets in between, and hang them on a clothesline using clothespins. When removing them from the press, try not to let the paper fold or bend.

2. Hang all the papers on the line.

3. Set up a fan to blow gently on the face of the sheets, not against the edges of the packs. Depending on sheet thickness, pressing strength, ambient temperature, and humidity, sheets can take anywhere from 12 to 48 hours to dry with this method.

Parting

1. After the bundles are dry, the sheets are ready to be peeled off. Test that the pack is completely dry by parting—separating—it in the center and feeling if the innermost sheet feels dry. If so, peel the felts and sheets off. I find it's much easier to separate the paper from the interfacing after the interfacing sheet is already peeled off the pack. Continue until each individual sheet of paper is free!

EVALUATE

Evaluate the dry paper. How does it look? Is it what you were expecting? Test the paper out by drawing or painting on it or using it for whatever purpose you intended. Does it work well for that purpose? How did the process work? What could have gone better? Use this information to continually improve your process and paper. Taking notes is a great tool!

NAME TAGS

If you're making paper with a group, make tiny paper name tags with permanent markers, then place them on the corners of the sheets before covering them with felts during couching. The name tags can be peeled away once the paper is dry and sorted. This also can be a great way to label samples or take notes about specific sheets as you're learning.

Papermaking Techniques

Now that you've successfully made your first batch of paper, we'll branch out by learning classic papermaking techniques, like using additives and colorants. Then we'll cover the artistic techniques you'll use in the projects.

Cooking Plant Fibers

If you harvest or purchase a raw plant material, it will need to be cooked in a caustic solution before beating or blending. Make sure to check the item description before purchasing a pulp so that you understand what fiber preparation the pulp needs.

Cooking removes the noncellulose portions of the plant, such as lignins and gums, and softens the fiber for beating. Each plant has an ideal processing procedure, but this is a generic cooking recipe to get started. Do the cooking in an outdoor area or somewhere with really great ventilation to avoid breathing the fumes and to avoid a mess. I like to use a propane burner outside and a stainless steel pot large enough for the fiber to float freely. Make sure none of the tools you use will later be used to prepare food.

FIBER COOKING RECIPE

MATERIALS

- Raw plant material
- Stainless steel pot
- Strainer
- Stirring utensil
- Outdoor propane burner and propane tank
- Soda ash
- Measuring cups
- Personal protective equipment: gloves, goggles

1. Make sure the plant fibers are completely dry. This ensures that they won't mold during processing. Take note of the dry weight of the material.

2. Put the plant fiber in the pot, then fill the pot with water, and add heat.

3. While wearing gloves and eye protection, measure ⅓ cup (79ml) of soda ash per 1 pound (450g) of dry fiber, and dissolve this into a separate small amount of hot water. Right before the water with the fiber comes to a boil, stir in the soda ash solution, being careful not to let it splash.

4. Allow the mixture to simmer for about two hours. Periodically stir the fiber. Then turn off the heat, and allow it to cool.

5. Drain off the dark liquid while wearing gloves and avoiding contact with your skin. I usually drain it into gravel near the cooking area. It should not be dumped down the drain if you have a septic system nor dumped onto plants or grass.

6. Rinse the fiber in a strainer, removing all traces of the soda ash. The fiber is now ready for pulping.

Papermaking Additives

Papermaking additives are substances that alter the properties of the pulp to create a desired effect in the resulting paper. I use pigments, a retention agent, sizing, and calcium carbonate in just about every batch.

The only two additives listed here that shouldn't be used in conjunction are a formation agent and a coagulant, which will counteract each other. Pigments should be added first, followed by a retention agent. Next, sizing and calcium carbonate can be added together. Finally, any other additives, like a coagulant or formation agent, can be added last.

PIGMENTS

The most reliable way to color pulp is to use aqueous dispersed pigments specifically made for papermaking, along with a retention agent. A retention agent will help ensure that the pigment sticks to the pulp instead of just floating in the water. Both these supplies are available from papermaking suppliers (like Carriage House Paper) in a variety of colors. I suggest getting a sample set, with small bottles of each color, to try them out. For safety, wear gloves to avoid prolonged contact between undiluted pigments and skin. Always add pigment before adding any other additives, like sizing. Retention agents do not work as well if other additives are already coating the pulp.

NOTE: BLEND COLORED PAPER
If you don't have access to aqueous dispersed pigments, add color to your paper by using recycled colored paper for your pulp. White office paper with black printing tends to blend to gray, but add in a few brightly colored scraps to get tints and shades.

ADDING PIGMENT

MATERIALS

- Prepared pulp in a bucket
- Aqueous dispersed pigments (at least one, any color)
- Measuring spoons, including very small spoons
- Retention agent
- Mixing cup
- Drill mixer or other mixing implement like a stirring stick

A

B

C

D

1. Prepare a batch of pulp. Make sure that the pulp is hydrated and has enough water that the pigment can flow.

2. Add 2 cups (0.5l) of water to a mixing cup. Shake the bottle of pigment to mix it up, then carefully open it. The colors are extremely concentrated, so even a tiny spill can make a large mess; be careful! Use a measuring spoon to scoop a small amount of pigment, then stir it into the water. If you are mixing multiple pigments to make a unique color, add them all together in the water. The look of the color in the water won't give an accurate idea of the saturation or shade in the final paper, but it will look like the hue of the final color. Keep mixing until it looks about right. **Ⓐ**

3. Add the pigment mixture into the pulp and stir vigorously. A drill with a paint mixing attachment works well for this in large batches, but a paint stirring stick, spoon, or a gloved hand can also work. **Ⓑ**–**Ⓓ**

4. Finally, add in the retention agent. The color cannot be changed after the retention agent is added, so make sure the hue is correct before reaching this step. Start with 2 cups (0.5l) of water in a mixing cup, then stir in the amount of retention agent needed (see Color Recipes, page 54). Add this mixture to the colored pulp, and mix vigorously. Allow it to sit for at least 10 minutes before adding other additives or dispersing the slurry in the vat. If a deeper, more saturated, or near black color is desired, it can be helpful to allow the pulp to sit longer—up to 8 hours for best results. See Color Testing (page 74) for more about fine-tuning the pigmenting procedure.

NOTE: RETENTION AGENT

Some retention agents come as powders. If you're using this kind, follow the directions to make it a solution before adding it to the pulp.

COLOR RECIPES

The following recipes will color enough pulp to yield 15 to 20 sheets of 8˝ × 10˝ (20 × 25cm) paper. Prepare 6 ounces (160g) of dry pulp using your preferred beating method, then color according to Adding Pigment (page 53). For bright, saturated colors, as shown, use white or near white pulp. The color recipes are created using aqueous dispersed pigments from Carriage House Paper.

The color recipes are divided into three levels that relate to the saturation and value of the colors. Add retention agent to every color based on the level of saturation:

- Level 1—use ½ tablespoon (7g) of retention agent

- Level 2—use ¾ tablespoon (10.5g) of retention agent

- Level 3—use 2 tablespoons (28g) of retention agent

Pink 1
6 drops
Quindo Red
6 drops Raw
Umber

Gray 1
3 drops Black
3 drops Violet

Yellow 1
⅛ tsp Yellow
Ochre

Orange 1
⅜ tsp Red
Iron Oxide
¼ tsp Yellow

Blue 1
¼ tsp Blue
Phthalo
½ tsp Raw
Umber

Pink 2
¾ tsp Quindo
Red
³/₁₆ tsp Burnt
Umber

Gray 2
³/₁₆ tsp Black
⅛ tsp Violet

Yellow 2
1½ tsp Yellow
Ochre

Orange 2
1 tbsp Red
Iron Oxide
1 tbsp Yellow

Blue 2
1½ tsp Blue
Phthalo
⅜ tsp Black

Pink 3
3 tbsp Quindo
Red
⅜ tsp Raw
Umber

Gray 3
1 tbsp Black

Yellow 3
2 tbsp Yellow
Ochre
¾ tsp Burnt
Umber

Orange 3
¾ tsp Red
Iron Oxide
1½ tbsp Burnt
Umber

Blue 3
2¼ tsp Blue
Phthalo
¾ tsp Black

Teal 1
¼ tsp Green
⅛ tsp Blue
Phthalo
⅛ tsp Raw
Umber

Avocado 1
3 drops Green
6 drops Burnt
Umber
¼ tsp Yellow
Ochre
6 drops Yellow

Jungle 1
6 drops
Yellow
¼ tsp Green
¼ tsp Burnt
Umber

Coral 1
¼ tsp Red
Iron Oxide
6 drops Red
⅛ tsp Yellow
Ochre

Sand 1
3 drops Burnt
Umber

Teal 2
2 tsp Green
¼ tsp Blue
Phthalo

Avocado 2
¼ tsp Green
¼ tsp Burnt
Umber
¼ tsp Yellow
Ochre
⅜ tsp Yellow

Jungle 2
1 tbsp Yellow
1½ tsp Green
¾ tsp Raw
Umber
¾ tsp Burnt
Umber

Coral 2
1 tbsp Red
Iron Oxide
⅛ tsp Red

Sand 2
⅛ tsp Burnt
Umber

Teal 3
1 tbsp Green
½ tsp Blue
Phthalo

Avocado 3
½ tsp Green
¾ tsp Burnt
Umber
1½ tsp Yellow

Jungle 3
1 tbsp Yellow
1½ tsp Green
1½ tsp Black

Coral 3
1 tbsp Red
Iron Oxide
2 tbsp Red
⅛ tsp Burnt
Umber

Sand 3
⅜ tsp Burnt
Umber
⅛ tsp Raw
Umber

SIZING

The exact amount and type of sizing needed depends on the final purpose of the paper and may take trial and error to dial in.

Internal Sizing

Internal sizing is added to the pulp before sheets are pulled. I use and recommend a ketene dimer emulsion available from Carriage House Paper as sizing. No matter what sizing you choose, follow the package instructions. After sheets are finished and dried, sizing does not affect the paper immediately. It may take up to a week to completely develop, so make sure you wait at least that long before testing the paper.

External Sizing

External sizing is applied to the surface of the paper sheets after they are dry. Sizing with gelatin is a popular and accessible option for external sizing.

ADDING INTERNAL SIZING

MATERIALS

- Prepared pulp in a bucket
- Sizing: suggest AKD (alkyl ketene dimer) liquid sizing
- Mixing cup
- Measuring spoons
- Water
- Drill mixer or other mixing implement like a stirring stick

1. Add 2 cups (0.5l) of water to a mixing cup. For each 1 pound (0.5kg) of dry pulp, use 1.5 tablespoons (21g) of sizing. Measure the sizing into the mixing cup and stir.

2. Add the mixture into the prepared pulp, and stir vigorously until combined.

ADDING EXTERNAL SIZING

MATERIALS

- Dry paper
- Powdered gelatin
- Heat-safe mixing cup
- Measuring spoons
- Water
- Wide paint brush
- Warming plate (optional)

1. Add 4 cups (1l) of water to a heat-safe mixing cup. Measure 1 tablespoon (14g) of gelatin powder, and stir the powder into the water. Let the mixture sit overnight to bloom.

2. The following day, heat the mixture in a microwave to a temperature that is hot but not boiling (approximately 190°F or 88°C). Heat for 20 seconds at a time, and stir in between. The mixture will become translucent, and the gelatin will dissolve. At this point, this mixture is a glue and will act as such anywhere it is allowed to dry or cool. The mixture must remain warm as you use it. I like to use a warming plate, but you could periodically pop it back in the microwave.

3. Saturate a large, wide brush with the gelatin solution, then paint it onto one side of the paper sheet. Make sure your brushstrokes go in only one direction. Add more gelatin to the brush, and apply another layer with perpendicular brushstrokes. This ensures an even coating with no unsized areas.

4. To dry, lay the sheets flat or hang them individually on a drying line. Remember, they are coated in a sticky glue, so they shouldn't be put in a dry box or stacked in any way until they are completely cool and dry. As soon as the gelatin is dry, the sheets are ready to go, and the sizing is activated immediately.

NOTE: TROUBLESHOOTING

If the sheets curl as they dry, wait for them to dry completely, then spritz them with water and stack them under a heavy weight to reflatten them.

NOTE: DIPPING IN SIZING

Sheets also can be dipped into the gelatin mixture in order to coat both sides. To do this, make the gelatin mixture twice as dilute: 8 cups (2l) of water to 1 tablespoon (14g) of gelatin.

Pour the hot mixture into a heated pan that is large enough to fit the sheets of paper. Submerge them one at a time, leaving each sheet in the solution for 5 seconds. Allow the extra solution to drip back into the pan, then hang each sheet to dry individually. Work quickly before the solution cools, or use a warming tray or other method to keep the pan warm while you work.

CALCIUM CARBONATE

Calcium carbonate is a kind of chalk that can be added to pulp as a buffer to protect the finished paper from future acids, whether they be from art media used on the paper or pollutants in the atmosphere that can be absorbed over time. In general, calcium carbonate makes paper more archival and longer lasting. Calcium carbonate should be added after pigment and a retention agent and at the same time as sizing.

ADDING CALCIUM CARBONATE

MATERIALS

- Prepared pulp
- Calcium carbonate powder
- Mixing cup
- Measuring spoons
- Water
- Drill mixer or other mixing implement

1. Add 2 cups (0.5l) of water to a mixing cup. For every dry pound (450g) of fiber, add 1 tablespoon (14g) of calcium carbonate. Stir well; the mixture will be cloudy.

2. Stir the solution vigorously into the pulp.

FORMATION AGENT

A formation agent is a goopy substance that can be added to the vat to slow down water drainage, thereby adding working time in the mould. Pulps that are excessively free (fast draining), heavy (want to sink to the bottom of the vat), or stringy and prone to tangling can be made easier to use with a formation agent. This additive can be especially useful for beginners who are just learning their vat person's shake. Formation agent powder can be purchased from papermaking suppliers.

ADDING A FORMATION AGENT

MATERIALS

- Prepared pulp in a bucket
- Formation agent powder
- Blender
- Strainer
- Measuring spoons
- Water
- Drill mixer or other mixing implement

1. Add 4 cups (1l) of water to a blender. Measure out ½ teaspoon (3g) of the formation agent powder. Put the lid on the blender, then plug it in and turn it on.

2. While the blender is running, slowly sprinkle the powder into the filler cap of the blender. Let the blender run for 20 seconds.

3. The mixture should become thick, goopy, and homogeneous. If particles or chunks are still visible, allow the mixture to sit and absorb for a few minutes, then blend further. Pour through a strainer before adding to the vat to remove any lumps.

4. Add 1 cup (0.25l) of the formation agent mixture to the vat full of pulp and water. Pull sheets normally. Every 5–10 sheets, add another cup of the formation agent mixture. If you want a higher concentration of formation agent, add more than one cup slowly; it is easy to add too much and end up with gross, goopy pulp that won't drain. Keep any leftover formation agent in a marked container in the refrigerator.

NOTE: CLEANUP

Formation agents can be extremely slippery if spilled. In the case of a spill, clean up immediately with hot water.

COAGULANTS

Coagulants cause the pulp to flocculate—form tiny lumps—allowing you to use multiple colors of pulp in a single vat. Multiple pulp colors can remain distinct instead of mixing together. PNS (polyacrylamide powder) coagulant is available at Carriage House Paper in powder form. The mixing process is identical to the process for a formation agent: ½ teaspoon (3g) of coagulant per 4 cups (1l) of water. A coagulant also can make a goopy mess if too much is added to pulp, so start slowly.

Coagulants work only in the presence of internal sizing or a retention agent. If a coagulant is added to pulp without one of these additives, it will act just as a formation agent.

ADDING A COAGULANT

MATERIALS

- Prepared pulp in color 1
- Prepared pulp in color 2
- PNS Coagulant powder
- Blender
- Strainer
- Measuring spoons
- Water
- Drill mixer or other mixing implement

1. Prepare and color pulp in at least two colors. Keep the colors in separate buckets.

2. In each pulp bucket, add a small amount of prepared coagulant. Stir by hand, and watch the pulp clump and separate. Add more or less coagulant solution based on the desired effect for your project. **Ⓐ**

3. Add a bit of each colored pulp to the vat, then pull the sheets as usual. The degree of vat stirring while pulling can create different effects. **Ⓑ**-**Ⓒ**

Pulp loosely stirred

Pulp vigorously stirred

Artistic Papermaking Techniques

INCLUSIONS

There are lots of materials you can add to the slurry or vat to create special effects in the final paper. Simply stir them in, then continue making paper as usual. As a general rule, you can add up to 10 percent of the dry weight in inclusions to the pulp without affecting the performance of the paper. Here's a nonexhaustive list of materials to try: gold foil, glitter, paper confetti, threads, small fabric bits.

EMBOSSING AND TEXTURE

During the pressing stage, it's easy to add materials on top of wet sheets to emboss or texture the paper. Any number of fabrics with a variety of textures (linen, damask, corduroy, fishnet, lace, quilt squares, etc.) are great additions and can easily be placed on top of wet sheets. Other thin objects can be used as well—cut shapes from paper, mylar, or foam or thread and string arranged into a pattern. Simply layer the material onto a sheet after it's couched, and stack as normal.

PAPER SCULPTURE

You can manipulate paper sheets to create more three-dimensional shapes or papers. Pull, couch, and press the sheets as usual. Then, instead of proceeding to drying, carefully peel the wet sheets off the felts. You can combine multiple sheets to make larger objects. Paper bowls are a great first project; lay the wet sheets over an existing bowl, and shape gently.

For any form, drape the sheet into the desired shape, and with your fingertips, a brush, or a sponge, stretch and work the sheet into the desired shape. Combine multiple sheets, or tear as needed. Allow overlap, and press the seams firmly with your fingertips to ensure they'll stick. This technique can also be used to cast shapes from linoleum or wood printmaking blocks. Place wet sheets on the surface, and use your fingertips or a brush to press the paper into the grooves.

LAYERING SHEETS

Wet sheets from the mould can be layered and combined during couching. Sheets combined during couching will dry as a unified sheet. Many of the techniques in this section can be used in conjunction with one another via layering.

REGISTRATION TEMPLATE FOR COUCHING

A registration template is a guide that helps you align layers while you couch. This technique can be used when the sheets need to align tightly on top of one another, and it is best used if all of your felts, towels, and sheets are the exact same size. You could also use this technique for all sheets if you have trouble aligning them on the post while you couch.

MATERIALS

- Sheet of EVA foam, at least 9″ × 12″ (22.9 × 30.5cm)
- Scissors
- Couching table
- Wet felt
- Pulled sheet in a mould and deckle (see Make Basic Sheets, page 38)

1. Cut a large, thick *L* shape from the EVA foam. Lay a wet felt on the couching table. **Ⓐ**

2. Align the *L* on the couching area, at one corner of the felt. Wet the foam, and press the foam down into the felt until surface tension holds it in place.

3. Hold the corner of the mould into the *L*, then couch as normal (see Couch Sheet, page 44).

4. Do not move the template, and for all subsequent sheets, again place the mould into the *L*, and couch. The layers will align perfectly as they stack. **Ⓑ**

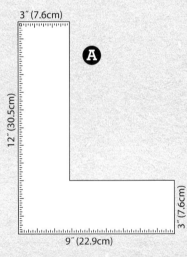

3″ (7.6cm)

12″ (30.5cm)

Ⓐ

3″ (7.6cm)

9″ (22.9cm)

Ⓑ

PAPERMAKER'S TEARS

Papermaker's tears form when stray drops of water from the papermaker's arms or deckle drop onto the surface of a wet sheet. They are traditionally considered imperfections. They leave a small, circular, thin area on the dry sheet that can be seen when held up to the light. But they also can be used artistically!

After the sheet is pulled, while it's still on the mould, simply drop water onto the surface. The amount of water, directionality, and force will affect the final result. Layer the sheet with tears directly over another sheet so they can be seen without being held up to the light. Experiment!

POURED PULP

For a painterly finished effect, dilute pulp with lots of water, then pour a cup of the slurry directly onto a piece of interfacing. Then couch a base sheet from the mould as normal on top of the same interfacing with poured pulp. Use colors in the poured pulp that will contrast with the base sheet.

GRADIENT SHEETS

You can achieve a gradient by dipping the mould only partially into the vat. Instead of using the usual vat person's shake, simply scoop the mould into the vat, keeping the back portion of the mould and deckle out of the slurry. Use a shallow angle for a longer gradient, or a more upright angle for a tidy transition. This technique works best with a thin slurry (lots of water and not a lot of pulp). Couch this sheet directly on top of a wet base sheet that has already been couched. Make sure the colors of the two pulps contrast.

PRESSED COLLAGE

You can collage pressed wet sheets onto wet, freshly couched sheets. They will dry as one sheet. This technique can be used to create collage-type pieces with various colors, as the pressed sheets can be hand manipulated (stretched, folded, torn) before they are layered with the fresh sheets.

This can be a good way to make sheets with multiple colors if you have space for only one vat at a time—just pre-make sheets in different colors, then collage them together onto wet sheets. Note that sheets that have been pressed but not dried should be used within two or three days. Keep them moist by topping the post with a wet towel or felt.

EVA Foam-Shaped Paper

Ethylene-vinyl acetate (EVA) foam is commonly sold as kids' fun foam in craft stores but is also available from cosplay and prop suppliers in more specialized sizes and thicknesses. This foam is durable and waterproof and can be used over and over again. It's great for shaping paper.

I recommend getting 6mm-thick sheets of EVA foam that are the size of your mould or a large roll to cut from if you need more flexibility. The thickness most commonly available is 3mm, which will work as you get started, if necessary. It can easily be cut with scissors or a craft knife, or a laser cutter, die cutter, and craft plotter can cut it.

USING STENCILS AND SHAPED DECKLES

Stencils allow you to form sheets in specific shapes. The stenciled pulp can be couched and layered on top of fresh sheets or used in conjunction with other techniques. Short fibers work best with stencils. I recommend a cotton linter pulp, finely beaten or blended for 30 seconds. A formation agent can be used to give the pulp more working time. See Patterned Paper (page 110) for an example of using stencils.

With a similar technique, you can use foam to make shaped deckles. This allows you to create a variety of paper shapes (round, oval, square, etc.) with one mould. You can also add foam pieces to a deckle with duct tape to create shapes (rounded corners, wavy edges, etc.) instead of cutting shapes out of a solid sheet of foam.

1. Cut the foam to the size and shape of the mould.

2. Cut shapes or patterns into the foam as desired for the stencil shape. Use rounded and curved shapes, with each area at least 1″ (2.5cm) across. Pulp fibers can get caught in tight corners and small spaces and then lift off with the deckle instead of remaining on the mould after pulling.

3. Use the foam instead of the deckle while pulling sheets. Paper will form only in the holes cut from the stencil.

DIVISION DECKLES

If you'd like to make many small sheets on one mould, use foam to create a division deckle. Cut the foam to the size and shape of the mould. Then measure out the desired size of smaller paper sheets, and mark them in a grid formation, leaving at least 1˝ (3cm) of foam between each sheet. Use the foam as a deckle, or attach to a wooden deckle with duct tape.

NOTE: WAYWARD PULP
If pulp is spilling behind the foam and in between the sheets or shapes, use duct tape on the top and bottom of the mould mesh in the same pattern as the foam.

ENVELOPES

For step-by-step instructions for creating an envelope, see the Card and Envelope project (page 114). Envelopes are great companions to paper. To make envelopes, find an envelope in a size and shape you like, then unglue and unfold it. Cut a piece of EVA foam to the size of the mould. Then trace the unfolded envelope shape onto the foam. Cut it out. Use the foam as a deckle, or tape the foam onto a deckle. Form sheets in the envelope shape as usual (pull, couch, press, dry).

When the sheets are dry, fold and glue them into envelope shapes. Refold the original envelope. Trace the rectangle shape onto cardboard or sturdy chipboard, and cut out. Then place the sturdy rectangle in the center of the dry, handmade paper. Score the paper around the rectangle, marking its shape. Remove the rectangle, and fold each flap up to make the envelope shape. Press and crease each fold.

If the paper overlaps in the inside corners, trim away excess paper with scissors or a craft knife. Apply glue (I prefer an archival glue stick, but some people use glue tape in a dispenser) to the side edges of the bottom flap, then fold it up onto the side flaps to adhere.

USING A DECKLE BOX

A deckle box is a kind of mould and deckle that is used for pouring sheets rather than pulling them. It is very useful for making samples since an entire vat doesn't need to be filled with pulp to make a single sheet. Arnold Grummer's sells a really great one with hook-and-loop tape straps.

1. Set the deckle box mould in a vat of plain water. The level of water in the vat should fill half of the deckle box mould.

2. Press the mould down to the bottom of the vat, as it will want to float. **A**

3. Pour pulp inside the deckle box. Mix it thoroughly to ensure an even distribution of pulp. **B**

4. Lift up the mould and deckle, and perform a vat person's shake as usual. **C**

5. Loosen the straps, and remove the deckle. Couch the paper onto a felt, and proceed as usual through the pressing and drying process. If you need to make a quick sample, dry using heat (see Heat Drying, page 24).

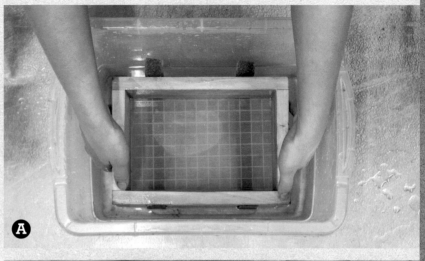

A

B

C

Papermaking Techniques   **67**

Professional Techniques

If you've made some paper and now you're thinking, "This could be better!" this chapter is for you! If you're looking for more consistency in your paper, sheet to sheet and batch to batch, if you're interested in selling your handmade paper, or if you just want to take your skills to the next level, read on!

Common Defects and Troubleshooting

PAPERMAKER'S TEARS

As discussed previously (page 63), papermaker's tears are the result of water droplets' falling onto the sheet while it's wet. They will show as paler circles (thin spots) and may have darker exterior rings. Prevent them by watching carefully where water drops are falling, especially when removing the deckle.

EDGE BURSTING

Edge bursting occurs when too much pressure is applied to a wet sheet. This is usually when the paper is pressed too quickly or with uneven distribution of pressure. It also can occur when too much force causes malformation to the sheets in the post underneath. Prevent edge bursting by using less pressure or applying pressure more slowly and evenly.

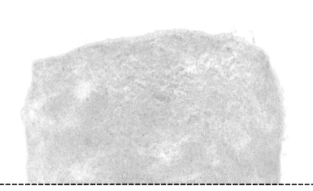 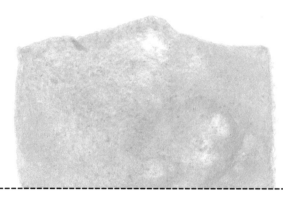

BLISTERS

When paper is being couched, especially the first sheet of a post, large air bubbles can occur under the sheet. When these pop and flatten, they leave a folded-over section around one edge of the bubble. Prevent these air bubbles by couching the first sheet of the post with more pressure or by using more couching towels under the post.

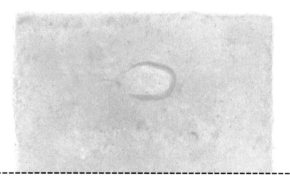

EDGE RUNNING

This imperfection occurs when sheets are couched too wet or too fast or when the post is too curved. As the couching motion is completed, the water in the sheet causes the final edge to wash out. The result is a sheet that is not rectangular and has a thin overhanging area.

LUMPS

Debris in the pulp can cause thick lumps in the finished paper—common culprits are rolled pills of dried paper, clumps of pigment, or strings from towels. Prevent debris by thoroughly cleaning all equipment and using good studio hygiene.

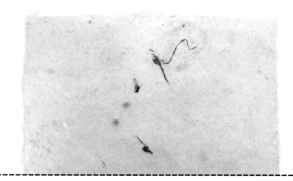

COCKLING

A wavy edge, called *cockling*, is caused by uneven drying, by stacking sheets that are not completely dry, or by applying uneven pressure to a stack of dry sheets. Sometimes it can be fixed by stacking the sheets under weights and reshuffling the order and direction of the sheets periodically. Prevent cockling by making sure the sheets are completely dry before peeling them and by stacking them with care.

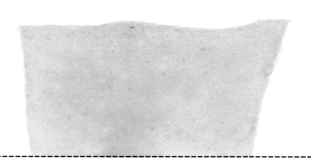

Paper Consistency

The weight of paper, measured in grams per square meter (GSM), is determined by the ratio of pulp to water in the vat. Other factors like the height of the deckle, how deeply the mould is scooped into the vat, and how much slurry is thrown off can also affect the weight of the paper. Each sheet that is pulled from the vat removes a certain amount of pulp and a certain amount of water. Making these variables homogeneous for each sheet will lead to paper that is a consistent weight sheet to sheet and batch to batch. Note that for all techniques, the larger the vat, the easier it is to maintain a consistent ratio.

MAKE SHEETS OF CONSISTENT THICKNESS

Water Out

The first variable to control is the water taken out with each pull. Ideally, half of the water from each sheet will drain back into the vat, and half will drain elsewhere. Usually, this can be achieved by doing the vat person's shake over the vat, then moving the mould away. During the few seconds of the shake, the water drains into the vat, and then the remainder of the water is drained away later as you complete the papermaking process. In my studio, the additional water drains on a table with gutters, but you could let it drain on a floor with a drain or into another vat or tray.

Pulp In

The second variable to control is how much pulp you add after each pull. This is determined by the starting ratio in the vat, the size of the sheets being made, and the target GSM (see Paper Weight, page 75). Speaking generally, you want to add the exact amount of pulp used in one sheet after pulling each sheet. One way to estimate this is to pull a sheet, ball up the pulp and rehydrate it to beater consistency, and measure the volume. Then you know exactly how to add the same volume of pulp after each sheet. Using trial and error, taking notes, and weighing the dry sheets after each session will help you perfect this process and pull consistent sheets.

PULP PER SHEET CALCULATION

If precision and a little math don't scare you, use the following calculations to determine the precise amount of pulp to add for a target paper weight. Please note that calculations work best in metric measurements, so that's what I'll be using. The pulp per sheet calculation needs the **target sheet weight** and the **beater concentration**.

BEATER CONCENTRATION

Start by determining the concentration of the pulp straight out of the beater. For instance, my beater holds 1,020 grams of dry pulp stuff and 115 liters of water. Divide the dry weight by the liquid to come up with the pulp concentration. For my beater, it is 8.87 grams per liter. If you're using a blender or other beating method, you can calculate this number by using the amount of dry fiber and water used in each batch.

Pulp Concentration Calculation

dry weight of pulp (grams) / water volume (liters)

TARGET SHEET WEIGHT

Use the target dry weight of the sheet to determine how much pulp to add. If you are making 8˝ × 10˝ sheets at 200 GSM, each sheet will weigh 10 grams (see Calculate Paper Weight, page 75).

Pulp per Sheet Calculation

target sheet weight (grams) / vat concentration (grams/liter)

10 grams / 8.87 grams per liter = 1.13 liter

The pulp per sheet calculation will give you the number of liters of prepared pulp (pulp and water) to add to the vat per sheet for the target sheet weight. In this example, 1.13 liters, or 1,130 milliliters, of slurry should be added to the vat after every sheet you pull. This will result in a consistent 8˝ × 10˝ sheet at 200 GSM.

But how much pulp should you add to the vat when you start? For the initial charging of the vat (adding slurry), I like to use the simple ratio of 10 parts water to 1 part pulp. In practice, it works best to first measure the amount of slurry that can fit in the vat comfortably, with the water level low enough that it doesn't splash with every pull but deep enough that the mould can be submerged easily. Then apply the ratio.

If the vat fits 45 liters of water, then add 4.5 liters of pulp. Of course, the beater concentration and the target thickness of the sheets will determine how accurate this ratio is, but it's a good starting place. In general, the amount of pulp added after each sheet matters more than the starting furnish, so don't overthink it! Just add pulp at a higher concentration for thicker sheets or if your beater concentration is much lower.

NOTE
The name tag trick from earlier (page 49) can be used as a learning tool! Make a bunch of tiny tags with numbers, one for each sheet of paper you plan to make. In a notebook, take notes as you work, with observations from each sheet. This might be something like "added 1 liter of pulp," "felt too light," or "maybe couched too fast." After the sheets are dry, compare the results to your notes.

Testing, Notebooks, and Recipes

Papermaking is equal parts art and science, and as with any scientific pursuit, record keeping is of utmost importance! If you want to be able to repeat batches and make a paper more than once, make sure your notes are clear and thorough.

Start by keeping records about every batch of pulp you make. Important details include

- Name and description of the material (source, condition, etc.)

- Starting weight of the material

- Any preprocessing (soaking, cutting, cooking, washing, etc.)

- Beating procedure and times (for a Hollander beater, this includes the time for loading and clearing as well as total beating time at each specific level)

- Amount and type of additives (sizing, calcium carbonate, pigments, retention agent, glitter, etc.)

- Notes about how the pulp looks, feels, and behaves

For extra thorough records, include a sample of the material before beating and a finished sheet of paper.

A three-ring binder with clear sheet protectors works perfectly for this, but a sketchbook with samples stapled in can work too. Keeping records will allow you to reproduce successful papers with ease.

MAKING PIGMENT RECIPES

Making a colored paper that matches something specific requires detailed testing and swatching.

I like to remove a small amount of the pigmented pulp, retain it with a retention agent, and dry a sample. This allows me to see the accurate color of the dry paper and compare it to my desired color without fixing the color to the entire batch. This process will also help you to build a color recipe book and swatch reference library that will be helpful for you and any clients in the future! Read more about pigment and retention agents in Using Papermaking Additives (page 52), and check out Color Recipes (page 54).

COLOR TESTING

MATERIALS

- Prepared pulp
- Aqueous dispersed pigments in desired colors
- Measuring spoons including very small spoons (recommended ¹⁄₆₄ tsp)
- Retention agent
- Mixing cup
- Deckle box mould
- Notebook and writing utensil
- Drill mixer or other mixing implement

1. Hydrate and prepare beaten pulp so that it is ready for color. Then add 2 cups (0.5l) of water to a mixing cup. Add pigment into the water. If you're mixing multiple pigments to make a color, add them all to the water.

2. Write down the amounts of each pigment added in a notebook. I love to use tiny ¹⁄₆₄ teaspoons to measure single drops for fine-tuned accuracy. Mix the pigment into the pulp.

3. To gather a sample, add 2 cups (0.5l) of water to a mixing cup, then scoop out 1 cup (0.25l) of pulp, and add it to the water. Add ½ tsp (2.5ml) of retention agent only to the mixing cup, and stir well. Let sit for about 10 minutes to allow the reaction to take place—for darker or more saturated colors, wait up to an hour.

4. Pour the pulp into a deckle box mould, and form a single sheet. Take note of any color that leeches from the pulp into the water—if the pulp is properly retained, only a whisper of color should come out in the water. If more color leaks into the water, for the next sample, add more retention agent, or let it retain longer before sampling.

5. Press and dry the sheet as usual, or speed up the process by drying it with heat (see Heat Drying, page 24).

6. When the sheet is completely dry, evaluate the color, and make adjustments to the rest of the wet pulp. If the color is too light, add more pigment in the same ratios as before. If the color is too bright, add the opposite color on the color wheel, or add brown or black to tone it down. Shift the hue by adding different pigments. For instance, if the green is too blue, add yellow. If the color is too dark, either add more pulp or drain the pigment out of the pulp and rinse. The color may stain a bit, but before retaining, almost all of the color can be rinsed off.

After making changes to the color, continue retaining, pulling, and drying samples until you have achieved the ideal color, and then add the retention agent to the entire batch and start making sheets.

TIP

Make a color swatch collection! I love to keep all successful color samples as possible future colors. I label each sheet with the date, and in a notebook, I keep track of the pigments used to make that color. Note that even when I'm working from an existing recipe, I always dry a test sheet before retaining a whole batch.

Grading and Sorting Paper

If you start selling paper, providing consistently high-quality paper sheets with no imperfections is crucial to keeping your customers coming back for more! The three-step process I use in my studio helps me to be sure that every sheet I sell meets quality standards. Grading paper is the process of determining its quality, which allows you to sort it into sellable batches.

PAPER WEIGHT

The first step is to understand and calculate the weight for a given sheet of paper. GSM is a standard way to calculate and express weight in the paper industry.

Calculate Paper Weight

weight (grams) / [length (meters) × width (meters)]

Convert the size of the sheet of paper to meters. For instance, an 8″ × 10″ sheet of paper is approximately 0.2 × 0.25 meters. One inch is approximately 0.03 meters, but an online calculator can easily make this conversion for you.

Weigh the sheet in grams using a scale. Let's say the sheet weighs 10 grams. Now calculate:

10 / (0.2 × 0.25) = 200 GSM

So the paper in this example is 200 GSM.

BASIS WEIGHT, OR PAPER POUNDS

In the United States, paper weights can be expressed in pounds, called the basis weight scale. However, this scale is inconsistent and confusing as it is determined by the type of paper in question. So on this scale, a 105 GSM sheet of paper intended for writing would be called 28 pounds, while a paper of the same GSM intended for book printing would be 70 pounds. For that reason, I don't recommend bothering with the basis weight system.

PAPER THICKNESS

Paper weight and paper thickness are not necessarily the same measure. Bulky, fluffy papers can be the same weight as dense, hard-packed paper. If paper of a specific thickness is desired, use a digital caliper to take thickness measurements. That said, if you use the same process to make all of your papers (same pulp, same pressing equipment), making heavier paper will mean making thicker paper.

Now that you know how to calculate paper weight, weigh each sheet in a batch to see if it falls within the expected weight range for the given paper type. Sort as needed.

In practice, if you sell a 200 GSM paper, as a buffer, you might allow 180–220 GSM papers to be sold at this weight. This is an acceptable range of about 9–11 grams for a piece of 8″ × 10″ paper.

Once I determined which types and sizes of paper I was planning to sell, I found it very helpful to make a chart of the various paper weights and sizes I offer and their grammage per sheet to make the sorting process easier. In my studio, sheets that are too light or too heavy are sold in bundles at a discounted price.

PICKING PAPER

The second step in the sorting process is called picking. Look at the surface of the sheet, and using a pair of sharp, pointed tweezers, pick off anything that shouldn't be there. This could be a stray thread, old paper left on the felts, lint, and so forth. You don't want visible debris on a sheet. Be sure to do this gently so that you don't damage the surface of the paper.

LOOK-THROUGH

The third step in the sorting process is to hold the sheet up to a light and look through it. Viewing papers like this will reveal many common formation defects. In my studio, if the sheet has any of the defects noted earlier in this chapter, it's sold as "imperfect" for a discounted price. If a sheet has any larger defects, like holes, it's called "broke," and it is recycled into new paper.

Once I've sorted the paper by weight, removed imperfections, and sorted out paper with defects, it's ready to be sold!

Pricing and Selling Paper

After making a couple thousand sheets to practice, you might decide you're ready to sell your paper. I use a basic pricing model:

1. Calculate the cost of all the single-use materials that go into a specific batch of paper. Include fibers, additives, and pigments (but not the whole cost of your studio setup).

2. Record how much time each part of the process takes, and assign an hourly wage for each step. For instance, sheet formation might be worth a higher wage than beating or fiber prep because it's more labor intensive or skilled. Multiply the wage of each step by the number of hours taken to complete that step.

3. Count how many sheets you make per specific batch. Add up the totals from Steps 1–2, and divide by the number of sheets. This is the cost per sheet. Multiply this by at least 2 before selling in order to make a profit. Remember that as a business, you will need to cover additional costs like studio expenses, new equipment,

cute packaging, paying an assistant, covering shipping, and other things.

4. Keep pricing consistent across multiple sizes by calculating the cost per square inch, then multiplying out for each size. To determine the cost per square inch, multiply the sheet length by the width, and then divide the cost by this number. If a 16″ × 20″ (40.6 × 50.8cm) sheet costs $10, the cost per square inch is 0.03125, so an 11″ × 14″ (27.9 × 35.6cm) sheet would be $4.81, and an 8″ × 10″ sheet would be $2.50 at the same rate.

5. Never undercharge for your labor, skill, and expertise!

Pricing Calculation

[cost of materials for batch + cost of labor for batch] / # of sheets per batch = cost per sheet

cost × 2 = price

USING A HOLLANDER BEATER

The Hollander beater is an incredible machine for hand papermakers, but it can be intimidating to operate! This section will get you up and running safely. Remember that you will likely need to train with a papermaker before starting to use a Hollander beater on your own.

SAFETY INFORMATION

Beaters are heavy industrial machines that can be dangerous to operate! Always plug a beater into an electrical outlet with a ground fault interrupter. Tie back loose fabric or hair that could get caught in the rotating parts. Never put your hands anywhere near the roll while it is running—add pulps and pull samples along the opposite side of the tub. After the beater is off, make sure the roll comes to a complete stop before removing the cover or touching the roll. Some beaters can be very loud and may require that the user wear hearing protection.

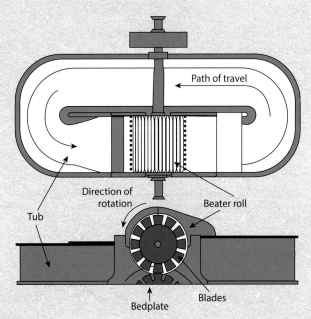

Continued on next page. ⟶

Loading a Hollander Beater

1. Weigh out dry fiber, and soak it in clean water for a couple of hours or overnight. Note the dry weight of each material in a record book before soaking.

2. Fill up the beater with cold water, almost to the water mark.

3. Move the roll off the bedplate at least 2˝ (5cm) into the starting position, and put on the roll cover and any other safety guards.

4. Plug the beater in, and turn it on.

5. Slowly add the pulp materials.

6. Use a paddle or wooden spoon to gently move the fibers toward the beater roll if they don't move in the water current.

7. Fibers will pass underneath the roll and be broken into smaller pieces. As the pieces become smaller, the fibers will float, and the stock will move more freely in the beater.

8. Over the next 20 minutes or so, slowly turn the beater roll down, one turn at a time.

9. When the roll is down to just one turn above the roll, it is considered loaded. Note this time in your record book.

Beating

Beating time depends entirely on the size of the beater and the speed of the stock rotation (largely determined by the speed of the motor). If you're using a beater for the first time, with no recipes for reference, do some tests to determine the proper beating time.

Start by beating for 20 minutes. Then perform a "doneness" test. Fill a small glass jar half full with water, then add a pinch of pulp and shake. If it is lumpy, continue beating. If the pulp looks like a fluffy cloud without clumps, it could be ready. Test further by removing enough pulp to make one sheet. Pull a sheet, or form using a deckle box mould.

Every 20 minutes thereafter, for up to 4 hours, remove more pulp, and make another test. Label the sheets with the beat time using name tags (see page 49). When the sheets are dry, see which sheet best suits your desires, and beat to this time in the future. In general, additional beating time will add more crispness and smoothness but will also increase drainage time for sheet formation and decrease tear resistance. Finding the right balance for your purposes is important. Test sample sheets in the ways you intend to use the finished papers—folding, painting, cutting, and so forth.

If you have an existing recipe, simply let the beater run for this set amount of time.

If the stock travel slows or stops, use a paddle or wooden spoon to push the pulp toward the beater roll. If this is a continual issue, consider adding more water or using less pulp stuff for the next batch, as it may be too dense for the motor.

Clearing

When the pulp is done beating, clear the batch, which removes knots and lumps. Raise the roll up about halfway, then allow it to run for about five minutes. This allows the beaten pulp to pass underneath the roll, slowly dispersing the knots. Then, over about 20 minutes, drop the roll back down to the level where it was beating, and then slowly raise it back to the starting position.

Unloading

After clearing, the pulp is ready to be removed from the beater. Turn off the machine, and unplug it. Remove the roll cover and any other safety guards. Position a bucket under the drain hole, and unplug the hole. Replug and repeat as necessary until all pulp is removed. Use a paddle or your hands to move pulp from stubborn areas and into the drain area.

Cleaning

After all the pulp has been removed, clean before the pulp has a chance to dry. If the roll lifts for cleaning, lift it, and gently spray it with a hose. Rinse or sponge the tub and any areas where pulp has stuck. Avoid spraying water onto the motor or pillar blocks. If the roll does not lift, a good way to clean it is to refill the beater with plain water, run it for a few minutes, then empty it again.

BEATING SHEET PULPS WITH A HOLLANDER BEATER

Sheet pulps are easy to beat in a Hollander beater using the above basic instructions. Simply soak the sheet pulps in water for a couple of hours or overnight, then tear them into fist-sized (or smaller) pieces before loading them into the beater. Note that when mixing various sheet pulps, they may have different ideal beating times. In this case, add the pulp that needs additional beating first, and then later raise the roll and add the second pulp.

BEATING OTHER PULPS WITH A HOLLANDER BEATER

Beating fabrics and plant fibers is much harder on the beater and may require some finesse. First, prepare any materials, and cut them into 1˝–2˝ (2.5–5cm) pieces or smaller. Make sure there are no long pieces or strings that can wrap around the roll and bind it. Plan to use a smaller quantity of pulp stuff than usual; if the beater usually holds 2 pounds (907g), start with 1.5 pounds (680g) of fabric or plant materials to avoid clogging the beater. Both fabric and plant materials beat better when combined with a small quantity of sheet pulp, which can help the heavier fibers float and rotate, especially to start.

Setting Up a Professional Studio

If you're spending a serious amount of time making paper, it might be time to consider upgrading your setup with the following recommendations. If you're just beginning, remember to check out Setting Up a Small Studio Space (page 18).

WATER MANAGEMENT

Floor Drains

As mentioned previously, working in an area with a drain in the floor can make cleaning very easy. Even so, keep in mind that the drain is for the removal of water only, and any pulp particles should be filtered out instead of sent down the drain. To avoid costly plumbing repairs, install a fine mesh drain cup in the drain, and empty it into the trash at the end of each day. Use a rubber floor squeegee to push water toward the drain.

When designing a new studio space, keep in mind that having several floor drains means that the flooring will be tilted to make the water flow into the drains. But studio equipment like Hollander beaters and hydraulic presses needs to be installed on a level surface to work properly.

Guttering Systems

A guttering system is an alternative to floor drains. A channel running along the front edge of your work table can drain all water from to a single location, like a bucket, which you can easily empty. All guttering should slope down slightly to the drain source. Regular household gutters can work, and adhesive drip rails intended for vehicles are another option, as are all kinds of DIY solutions. I'd recommend guttering around your press first, as it creates the largest volume of water, then around the formation table or couching area. If you have a Hollander beater, a draining cart or table with a drain system can be helpful there as well.

Pumping Systems

If you're using guttering to channel all the water to a single location, the next improvement would be a pumping system to move the water to a drain, eliminating the need to lift and dump buckets. The most important factor to consider in a pump system is which water will contain pulp residue. Water coming out of a press will be clean and free of pulp, but water coming from most other areas will contain stray bits of pulp.

For clean water, a condensate pump (used for moving condensation from air conditioners or dehumidifiers) or a water pump meant for a fountain is a great option. For water with any amount of pulp, use a sump pump or trash pump—intended to move water in a flooding situation—which can handle small debris.

With any pump, use clear PEX piping so you can see if there are clogs or algae growth. The piping should be arranged to move the water directly above the pump with a downward angle so water is never sitting in the pipes. In my studio, several pumps fill one large basin that contains a sturdy trash pump. When the basin fills, the pump turns on and pumps into a large main drain. You can set up a water reuse system using these same ideas and channeling water into a filtration system or a holding tank.

Hose

A hose is the most useful and efficient method for filling vats and beaters. If possible, install a hose with hot and cold water. Cold water should be used in the beater, but warm or hot water can be used in vats for the papermaker's comfort, especially in the winter. Invest in a high-quality, heavy-duty hose to prevent frustration from kinking. If the hose is in a high-traffic area, consider using a retractable hose holder or other storage system to prevent tripping. Fire hose nozzles work best for filling vats as they don't have to be held like a trigger nozzle and they are heavy enough to stay in vats without clips. I also find them to be more durable and long-lasting than other nozzles.

Sink

The sink is the main area for washing. I recommend a single compartment industrial sink with a drain board. The drainboard becomes a useful area for working with pigments and additives, and it can be easily rinsed off into the sink at cleanup. Measuring cups and buckets can be left on the drain board to dry, preventing water puddles elsewhere. A faucet with a sprayer attachment can be very helpful for cleaning. In the drain, use a simple mesh strainer cup to catch all pulp and debris.

ERGONOMICS AND WORKING COMFORT

If you intend to make paper on a regular basis for work, consider ergonomics and comfort for your body. Papermaking can be heavy and repetitive work.

Couching stands and formation area tables should be positioned 7″–10″ (18–25cm) below the elbow or hit at the upper thigh region. This height ensures that you can apply downward force while couching without bending or stooping. The top of the vat should hit at the hip bones, and the vat should be of a sturdy material that can support the weight of the body during forming. Your feet should be able to fit underneath the vat or the table it's on. For a studio space that is shared with multiple papermakers, consider designing the furniture to be adjustable in height to suit each maker.

When making paper, always use smooth and even motions. Jerking and twisting motions should be avoided at all times. Keep tension out of the hands by only loosely holding the mould, not grasping it tightly. Keep the knees loose and unlocked.

Whenever possible, use tools to assist with heavy lifting. Move buckets around on wheeled dollies. Move the post with lift tables and carts, or arrange your studio so you can slide materials from one area to another.

Papermaking is a standing craft, and the feet and legs can suffer. If you're building a new studio space, consider installing a floor made of a soft material like floating wood covered in waterproof linoleum or vinyl. In my new second-floor space, I used a roll of seamless linoleum flooring with waterproof edging to create what looks like a giant tray. If the floors are concrete, invest in a high-quality antifatigue mat for each area you regularly stand in or walk through. Quality waterproof shoes are also a lifesaver. Ditch the foam clog shoes, rubber flip flops, or heavy rain boots in favor of lightweight strap-on sport sandals or water-resistant sneakers with insoles.

EXERCISE

The body is your most important tool, and over time, you can do a lot to enhance your working ease and reduce the risk of injury. Work to build strength in the ranges of motion needed for papermaking.

With gym machines or weights, practice hip-hinging exercises like deadlifts and good mornings to strengthen the lower back and backs of the legs. Exercises that strengthen the back muscles, like variations of bent-over rows, also help. These back exercises will strengthen the muscles needed for pulling the mould through the vat.

Ventral raises will strengthen the shoulders and abdominal muscles to make it easier to hold the mould during draining. To build strength for walking with heavy buckets and posts, use exercises like waiter's carries, plate carries, and farmer's carries.

Before papermaking, start the day with warm-up exercises, and afterward, finish with a stretching routine. A good warm-up should include cardiovascular exercises to get the blood pumping and movements that mimic papermaking. This should reduce stiffness and prepare the body for work. A walk around the block, walking lunges, and fake papermaking motions should do the trick. At the end of the day, stretch all the muscles that you used. For particular aches and pains, I work with my local physical therapist or yoga instructor to develop a personalized routine.

PROJECTS

For all projects, you'll need a basic papermaking studio setup as described in Tools and Supplies (page 18) and Make Basic Sheets (page 38). This includes a way to prepare pulp; a vat; a mould and deckle; felts; a couching table; a press; and other small tools like buckets, mixing cups, and towels.

You'll need pulp prepared as noted in each project. All samples shown are made from a mixture of abaca and cotton sheet pulps prepared in a Hollander beater, but you can use any type of pulp you prefer and have access to. Color the pulp according to Color Recipes (page 54). Refer to Papermaking Additives (page 52) for reminders about how to test colors and use additives. All projects and stencils are designed for use with a mould and deckle measuring around 8˝ × 10˝ (20 × 25cm).

LINEN-TEXTURED PAPER

The project will make paper with a woven surface texture. You can use the same technique with any fabric to emboss texture onto the sheets. This project will make 10 sheets of linen paper.

MATERIALS

- ½ batch of pulp in Sand 3 color
- 10 pieces of woven textured linen fabric cut to 9″ × 12″ (23 × 30.5cm)

Additives Required to Prepare Pulp

Burnt Umber aqueous dispersed pigment

Raw Umber aqueous dispersed pigment

Retention agent

Techniques Needed

Color Recipes, page 54

Make Basic Sheets, page 38

Embossing and Texture, page 62

Make the Paper

1. Prepare the vat with the Sand 3 pulp.

2. Pull and couch 1 sheet of paper.

3. Place the linen fabric on top of the paper sheet in the couching area. Cover with a felt. **Ⓐ**

4. Repeat Steps 2–3 until you have five sheets. Lay down a towel to separate the post, then repeat five more times until all the fabric is used and 10 sheets are in the post.

5. Press and dry the post, then peel the linen away from each sheet once the paper is dry. **Ⓑ**

Ⓐ

Ⓑ

ROSE GOLD FOIL PAPER

The project will make paper with beautiful rose gold flecks throughout. It's perfect for weddings and classy handmade invitations or place settings. You can make variations by mixing different colored pulps with different colored metal leaf. This project will make 15–20 sheets.

MATERIALS

- 1 batch of pulp in Orange 1
- Imitation rose gold or copper foil schabin flakes

Additives Required to Prepare Pulp

Red Iron Oxide aqueous dispersed pigment

Yellow aqueous dispersed pigment

Retention agent

Techniques Needed

Color Recipes, page 54

Make Basic Sheets, page 38

Inclusions, page 61

Make the Paper

1. Prepare the vat with Orange 1 pulp.

2. Add the foil flakes to the vat.

3. Pull sheets, couch them, and repeat until all the pulp is used. Sprinkle more flakes into the vat as you go if they become sparse. **B**

4. Press and dry the sheets as usual. **C**

THREAD INCLUSION PAPER

This project will make a fun, festive paper with colorful bits of thread swirling throughout. Mix it up by trying a different color of pulp or curating a specific color palette of thread. I like to recycle floss scraps after I finish an embroidery project. This recipe makes 15–20 sheets.

MATERIALS

- 1 batch of pulp in Pink 1
- Scraps of embroidery floss or cotton thread in any colors
- Scissors

Additives Required to Prepare Pulp

Quindo Red aqueous dispersed pigment

Raw Umber aqueous dispersed pigment

Retention Agent

Techniques Needed

Color Recipes, page 54

Make Basic Sheets, page 38

Inclusions, page 61

Make the Paper

1. Collect scrap embroidery floss, and cut it into pieces to 1″–3″ (2.5–7.5cm). **A**

2. Prepare the vat with Pink 1 pulp.

3. Add the pieces of embroidery floss to the vat. **B**

4. Pull sheets, couch them, and repeat until all the pulp is used. **C**

5. Press and dry the sheets as usual. **D**

CONFETTI PAPER

Confetti paper is great no matter the occasion because it's so customizable. In this project, you'll pull standard sheets and cut them into confetti. These inclusions are then one of a kind, and every part of this paper is handmade by you. Cut wavy shapes for an organic and elegant look, or choose more geometric shapes for something more playful. I chose to hand-cut geometric shapes. This recipe makes 15–20 sheets.

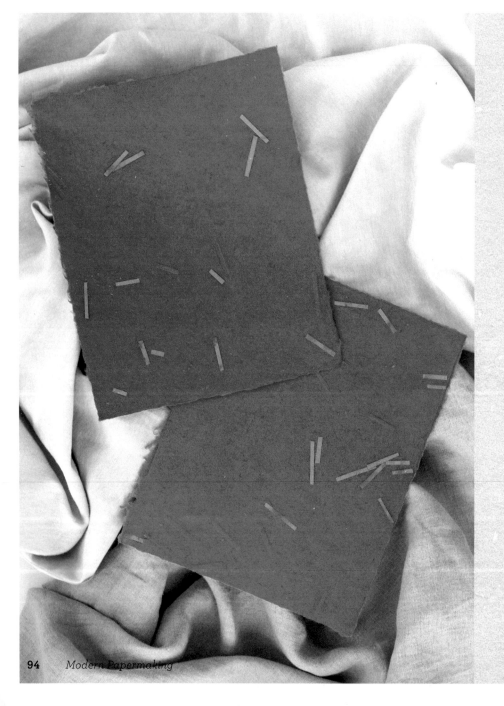

MATERIALS

- 1 batch of pulp in Coral 2
- ½ batch of pulp in Coral 1
- ½ batch of pulp in Yellow 2
- Scissors or other cutting tool

Additives Required to Prepare Pulp

Red Iron Oxide aqueous dispersed pigment

Red aqueous dispersed pigment

Yellow Ochre aqueous dispersed pigment

Retention agent

Techniques Needed

Color Recipes, page 54

Make Basic Sheets, page 38

Inclusions, page 61

Make the Paper

1. Prepare the vat with Coral 1 pulp. Pull five sheets, and couch them. Press and dry as usual.

2. Prepare the cleaned vat (or a second vat) with Yellow 2 pulp. Pull five sheets, and couch. Press and dry as usual.

3. When dry (after at least one day), cut all 10 papers into shaped confetti, with each shape smaller than 1˝ (2.5cm). For this example, I used scissors, but laser cutters, die cutters, craft plotters, and paper punches will all work.

4. Prepare a vat with Coral 2 pulp.

5. Stir the confetti shapes into the vat. Pull sheets, couch them, and repeat until all the pulp is used. **Ⓐ** **Ⓑ**

6. Press and dry the sheets as usual. **Ⓒ**

Ⓐ

Ⓑ

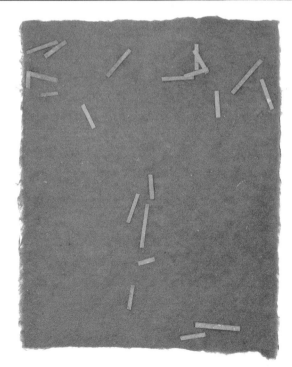

Ⓒ

ARCH-SHAPED PAPER

This project creates an elegant shaped paper with two rounded corners. It's great as a starting canvas for painting or drawing thanks to the eye-catching organic shape. This recipe makes 15–20 sheets.

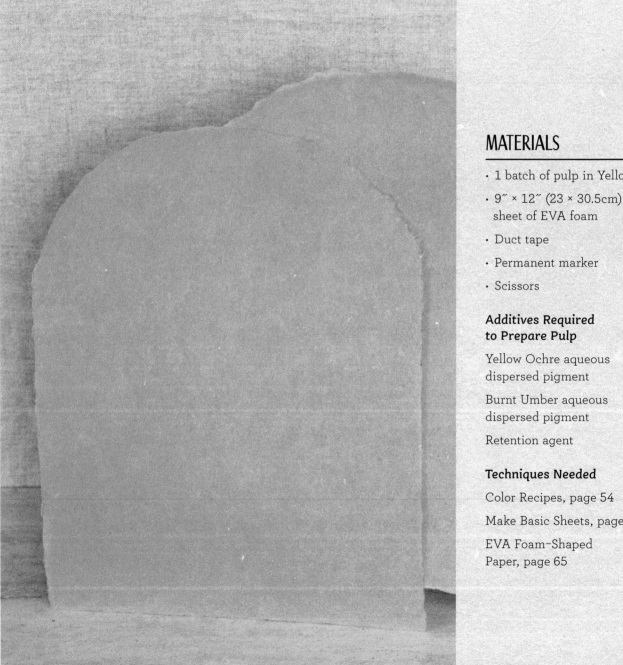

MATERIALS

- 1 batch of pulp in Yellow 3
- 9″ × 12″ (23 × 30.5cm) sheet of EVA foam
- Duct tape
- Permanent marker
- Scissors

Additives Required to Prepare Pulp

Yellow Ochre aqueous dispersed pigment

Burnt Umber aqueous dispersed pigment

Retention agent

Techniques Needed

Color Recipes, page 54

Make Basic Sheets, page 38

EVA Foam-Shaped Paper, page 65

Make the Paper

1. Prepare an arch-shaped deckle. Trace the inside edge of the deckle onto the foam with a permanent marker, then round the top two corners. **Ⓐ**

2. Cut out the arch shape, keeping the outside piece intact. Set aside the middle piece. **Ⓑ**

3. Using duct tape, attach the outline of the arch to the deckle. **Ⓒ**

4. Prepare the vat with Yellow 3 pulp.

5. Pull sheets, couch them, and repeat until all the pulp is used. **Ⓓ**

6. Press and dry the sheets as usual. **Ⓔ**

7. Remove the duct tape from the deckle, and clean well. The foam arch can be dried and saved for future use.

Arch-Shaped Paper   **97**

PLACE CARDS

This project makes several small papers on a single mould. These small sheets can be used as place cards or business cards. Switch it up with other colors of pulp for a rainbow of tiny sheets. The project makes 60–120 cards.

MATERIALS

- 1 batch of pulp in Pink 3
- 9˝ × 12˝ (20 × 25cm) sheet of EVA foam
- Stiff cardboard or card stock
- Scissors or craft knife

Additives Required to Prepare Pulp

Quindo Red aqueous dispersed pigment

Raw Umber aqueous dispersed pigment

Retention agent

Techniques Needed

Color Recipes, page 54

Make Basic Sheets, page 38

Division Deckles, page 66

Make the Paper

1. Trace the deckle onto EVA foam using a permanent marker, marking both the exterior and the interior edges of the frame. Cut the foam on the exterior line. **Ⓐ**

2. Cut a 3.5˝ × 2˝ (9 × 5cm) rectangle template from the cardboard or card stock.

3. Match the template to one corner of the deckle shape on the foam. Trace the rectangle onto the foam. **Ⓑ**

4. Move the template over 1˝ (2.5cm), and then trace another rectangle. Continue moving and tracing the template, making sure to leave 1˝ (2.5cm) between each rectangle shape. You should be able to fit 4–6, depending on the exact size of your mould. **Ⓒ**

5. Carefully cut out all the place card shapes from the foam using scissors or a craft knife, keeping the space around the rectangles intact. Round the corners slightly to allow the pulp to release easily. **Ⓓ**

6. Prepare a vat with Pink 3 pulp.

7. Using the EVA division as a deckle instead of the usual deckle, pull sheets, couch them, and repeat until all the pulp is used. **Ⓔ**

8. Press and dry the sheets as usual. **Ⓕ**

Ⓐ

Ⓑ

Ⓒ

Ⓓ

Ⓔ

Ⓕ

MOON PAPER

This project layers two sheets to create paper with a realistic cratered moon pattern. It's a stunning paper that makes use of a papermaking technique traditionally considered an imperfection—papermaker's tears. This project makes 15–20 sheets.

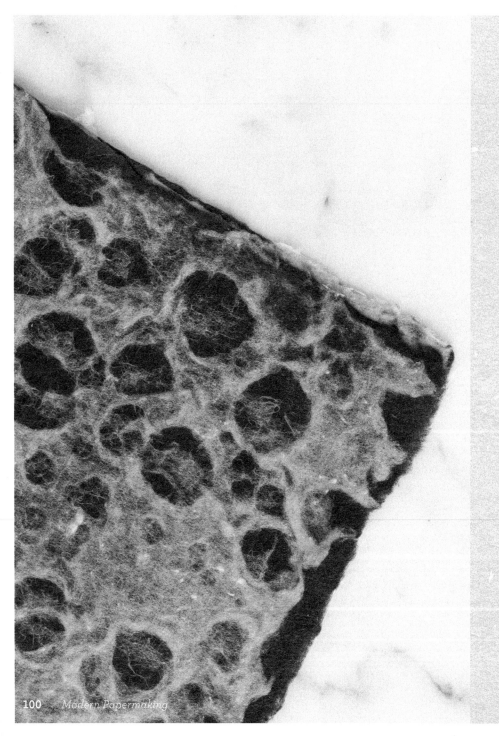

MATERIALS

- 1 batch of pulp in Gray 3
- ½ batch of pulp in Gray 1
- 2 vats
- Couching table with registration template

Additives Required to Prepare Pulp

Black aqueous dispersed pigment

Violet aqueous dispersed pigment

Retention agent

Techniques Needed

Color Recipes, page 54

Make Basic Sheets, page 38

Papermaker's Tears, page 63

Layering Sheets, page 62

Registration Template for Couching, page 63

Make the Paper

1. Prepare two vats: the first with Gray 3 pulp and the second with a very thin slurry of Gray 1 pulp.

2. Pull a Gray 3 sheet, and couch it onto the felt using the *L* registration method.

3. Pull a Gray 1 sheet. It should be thin and translucent.

4. Alter the Gray 1 sheet with papermaker's tears. Using a hose or cup of water, intentionally drip water onto the sheet while it is still on the mould. Hold the mould horizontally, and drip the water straight down in single drops, creating round papermaker's tears. Allow some drops to drip into the same area to create larger divots.

5. Align the mould with the L, and couch the Gray 1 sheet on top of the Gray 3 sheet. This will now dry as one sheet.

6. Repeat Steps 2–5 until all the pulp is used.

7. Press and dry the sheets as usual.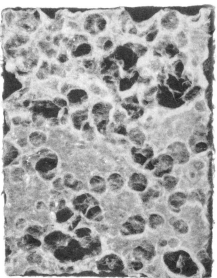

WAVE PAPER

This project combines three layers to create a paper that looks like an ocean wave washing up on the beach. It uses papermaker's tears and a gradient to modify the look of the paper. This project makes 15–20 sheets.

MATERIALS

- ½ batch of pulp in Sand 1
- ½ batch of pulp in Teal 1
- 1 batch of pulp in Sand 2
- 3 vats
- Registration template

Additives Required to Prepare Pulp

Burnt Umber aqueous dispersed pigment

Green aqueous dispersed pigment

Phthalo Blue aqueous dispersed pigment

Raw Umber aqueous dispersed pigment

Retention agent

Techniques Needed

Color Recipes, page 54

Make Basic Sheets, page 38

Gradient Sheets, page 64

Papermaker's Tears, page 63

Layering Sheets, page 62

Registration Template for Couching, page 63

Make the Paper

1. Prepare three vats. Prepare the first vat with the Sand 2 pulp. Prepare the second vat with Teal 2 pulp. Prepare the third vat with a very thin slurry of Sand 1 pulp.

2. Pull a sheet of Sand 2 pulp, and couch it onto the felt using the *L* registration method.

3. Pull a sheet of Teal 3 pulp using the gradient technique, inserting the mould halfway into the vat. Couch the gradient sheet on top of the Sand 1 sheet. **Ⓐ**

4. Pull a very thin sheet of Sand 1 pulp. Alter this sheet with papermaker's tears. Using a hose or cup of water, intentionally drip water onto the sheet while it's still on the mould. Hold the mould at a 45° angle, and pour the water drops from top to bottom, forming the pulp into rolls and mounds. **Ⓑ**

5. Couch the Sand 1 sheet on top of the other 2 sheets. This is now 1 sheet.

6. Repeat Steps 2–5 until all the pulp is used.

7. Press and dry the sheets as usual. **Ⓒ**

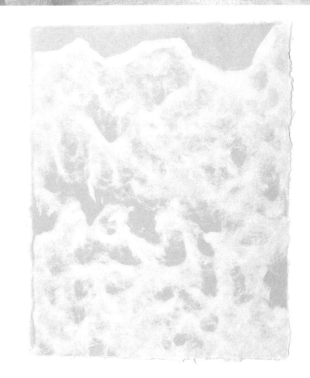

MOSS PAPER

This project uses coagulant to create papers with multiple colored speckles in one sheet. After you try the moss colorway, experiment with other color combinations to make variations. This project makes 30–40 sheets.

MATERIALS

- ½ batch of pulp in Jungle 1
- ½ batch of pulp in Jungle 2
- ½ batch of pulp in Jungle 3
- ½ batch of pulp in Orange 3

Additives Required to Prepare Pulp

Yellow aqueous dispersed pigment

Green aqueous dispersed pigment

Burnt Umber aqueous dispersed pigment

Raw Umber aqueous dispersed pigment

Black aqueous dispersed pigment

Red Iron Oxide aqueous dispersed pigment

Retention agent

PNS coagulant

Techniques Needed

Color Recipes, page 54

Make Basic Sheets, page 38

Coagulants, page 60

Make the Paper

1. Mix the coagulant according to the instructions in Adding a Coagulant (page 60).

2. Keeping the four pulp colors in separate buckets, mix coagulant into each pulp. Start with 1 tablespoon (14g) per bucket. The pulp should become chunky and separate; if it does not, add more coagulant until you notice this reaction. **Ⓐ**

3. Fill one vat as usual, using an equal portion of each color

4. Pull sheets, couch them, and repeat until all the pulp is used. **Ⓑ**

5. Press and dry the sheets as usual. **Ⓒ**

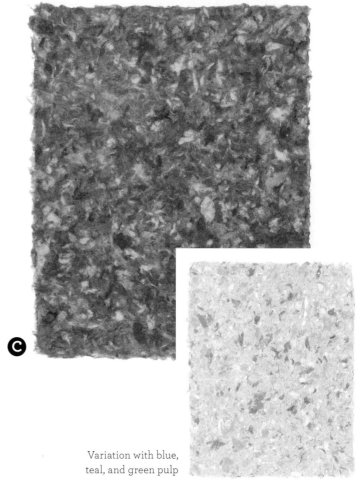

Variation with blue, teal, and green pulp

GLACIER PAPER

In this project, you will rip wet sheets by hand to create layered shapes reminiscent of glaciers. Try experimenting with tearing different shapes and using different color palettes. This project makes 15–20 sheets.

MATERIALS

- 1 batch of pulp in Blue 1
- ½ batch of pulp in Blue 2
- ½ batch of pulp in Blue 3
- ½ batch of pulp in Teal 2
- ½ batch of pulp in Orange 2
- ½ batch of pulp in Coral 3
- 8˝ × 10˝ (20 × 25cm) deckle box (recommended but optional)

Additives Required to Prepare Pulp

Blue Phthalo aqueous dispersed pigment

Raw Umber aqueous dispersed pigment

Black aqueous dispersed pigment

Green aqueous dispersed pigment

Red Iron Oxide aqueous dispersed pigment

Yellow aqueous dispersed pigment

Red aqueous dispersed pigment

Burnt Umber aqueous dispersed pigment

Retention agent

Techniques Needed

Color Recipes, page 54

Make Basic Sheets, page 38

Pressed Collage, page 64

Using a Deckle Box, page 67

Make the Paper

1. Prepare pulp in each color. I recommend using a deckle box mould in Step 2 to save on cleanup time and waste, but if that's not an option for you, a traditional mould and deckle setup will work.

2. Pull and couch 5 sheets in each of the following colors: Blue 2, Blue 3, Teal 2, Orange 2, and Coral 3. Press, but don't dry.

3. Prepare a vat with the Blue 1 pulp.

4. Pull and couch 1 sheet.

5. Tear each of the pressed sheets into 4 approximately equal strips. You should have 5 sheets worth of strips in every color except Blue 1. Layer the colored strips onto the Blue 1 base sheet while it's still wet. Leave a strip of the base paper uncovered at top and bottom, and make sure all the other strips overlap.

6. Top the layered glacier composition with a felt, then couch another sheet of Blue 1 on top. Repeat Step 5 until supplies run out.

7. Press and dry the layered sheets as usual.

LAYERED COLLAGE PAPER

This project uses wet paper "stickers" that are collaged onto a base sheet. Experiment with arranging the pieces into novel compositions. This project makes 15–20 sheets.

MATERIALS

- ½ batch of pulp in Gray 2
- ½ batch of pulp in Pink 2
- ½ batch of pulp in Avocado 1
- 1 batch of pulp in Avocado 3
- 9″ × 12″ (23 × 30.5cm) sheet of EVA foam
- Craft knife

Additives Required to Prepare Pulp

Black aqueous dispersed pigment

Violet aqueous dispersed pigment

Quindo Red aqueous dispersed pigment

Burnt Umber aqueous dispersed pigment

Green aqueous dispersed pigment

Yellow Ochre aqueous dispersed pigment

Yellow aqueous dispersed pigment

Retention agent

Techniques Needed

Color Recipes, page 54

Make Basic Sheets, page 38

Pressed Collage, page 64

Using Stencils and Shaped Deckles, page 65

Collage Template, page 116

Preparing the Stencil Deckle

1. Trace the Collage Template (page 116) onto a piece of paper.

2. Tape the template, centered, onto a 9˝ × 12˝ (23 × 30.5cm) sheet of EVA foam.

3. Using a craft knife, cut through the paper and foam on the lines to create the stencil deckle.

4. Remove paper.

5. Trim the edge of the EVA foam to fit the mould as needed.

Make the Paper

1. Prepare a vat of Gray 2 pulp, and using the stencil deckle, pull 10 sheets. Couch and press the sheets as usual, but do not allow them to dry.

2. Repeat Step 1 with Pink 2 and then Avocado 1. Set additional 2 posts of wet sheets aside.

3. Prepare a vat of Avocado 3.

4. With the mould and a regular deckle, pull 1 sheet of Avocado 3, and couch it.

5. From the wet posts of pressed stencil shapes, carefully peel the shapes from the interfacing. Place them on the Avocado 3 base sheet in a collage fashion, however you desire. The shapes can overlap and be layered, or be placed with space between them. Repeat until you have used all the shapes or Avocado 3 pulp.

6. Press and dry the collaged sheets as usual.

PATTERNED PAPER

This project makes a patterned paper with whimsical organic shapes. The project makes an abstract design in bright colors, but the technique also can be used to make patterns that are more structured or representative, like animal print or polka dots. The project makes 15–20 sheets.

MATERIALS

- 1 batch of pulp in Avocado 2
- 1 batch of pulp in Teal 3
- 9˝ × 12˝ (23 × 30.5cm) sheet of EVA foam
- Couching table with registration template
- 2 vats
- Scissors
- Permanant marker

Additives Required to Prepare Pulp

Green aqueous dispersed pigment

Burnt Umber aqueous dispersed pigment

Yellow aqueous dispersed pigment

Phthalo Blue aqueous dispersed pigment

Yellow ochre aqueous dispersed pigment

Retention Agent

Techniques Needed

Color Recipes, page 54

Make Basic Sheets, page 38

Layering Sheets, page 62

Using Stencils and Shaped Deckles, page 65

Registration Template for Couching, page 63

Pattern Template, page 117

Preparing the Stencil Deckle

1. Trace the Pattern Template (page 117) onto a piece of paper.

2. Cut out the shapes with scissors, and trace them onto the sheet of EVA foam with permanant marker.

3. Using scissors, cut the shapes out of the foam on the lines to create the stencil deckle.

4. Trim the edge of the EVA foam to fit the mould as needed.

Making the Paper

1. Prepare one vat with Avocado 2 pulp. Prepare a second vat with Teal 3 pulp.

2. Using a mould and regular deckle, pull a sheet of Avocado 2 paper, and couch using the *L* registration technique.

3. Using the stencil as a deckle, pull 1 sheet of the Teal 3 paper.

4. Couch the patterned paper on top of the base sheet. This is now 1 sheet.

5. Continue Steps 2–4 until all pulp is used.

6. Press and dry the sheets as usual.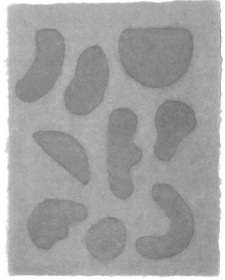

DAYDREAM PAPER

This project uses poured pulp to create beautiful, painterly sheets. Poured pulp creates unexpected and dynamic finished results that make each sheet unique. This project makes 15–20 sheets.

MATERIALS

- ½ batch of pulp in Pink 1
- ½ batch of pulp in Teal 1
- ½ batch of pulp in Avocado 3
- ½ batch of pulp in Coral 2
- 1 batch of pulp in Sand 1
- Small cups for pouring

Additives Required to Prepare Pulp

Quindo Red aqueous dispersed pigment

Raw Umber aqueous dispersed pigment

Phthalo Blue aqueous dispersed pigment

Green aqueous dispersed pigment

Yellow aqueous dispersed pigment

Burnt Umber aqueous dispersed pigment

Red Iron Oxide aqueous dispersed pigment

Red aqueous dispersed pigment

Retention agent

Techniques Needed

Color Recipes, page 54

Make Basic Sheets, page 38

Poured Pulp, page 64

Make the Paper

1. Prepare half batches of pulp in Sand 1, Teal 1, Avocado 3, and Coral 2. Keep in separate containers. Dilute with 3 times the usual amount of water.

2. Prepare a vat of the Pink 1 pulp.

3. Using the small cups, pour a small amount of each of the diluted colored pulps onto a piece of interfacing on the couching table. The pouring technique and the order in which they are poured will affect the finished look, so pay attention to the order and places you pour. Experiment with different techniques, and take notes for future batches. **Ⓐ**

4. Pull 1 sheet from the Pink 1 vat, and couch it over the poured pulps. Cover with interfacing.

5. Repeat Steps 3–4 until all Pink 1 pulp is used.

6. Press and dry the sheets as usual. **Ⓑ**

Ⓐ

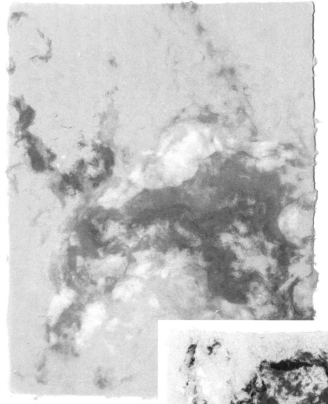

Ⓑ

Variation with black, white, and gray pulps

CARD AND ENVELOPE

This project makes a set of very cute and very tiny envelopes with matching folded cards. Send and leave adorable notes for loved ones, or use as favors and gift tags. Makes 20–25 folded cards with matching envelopes.

MATERIALS

- Pulp in Yellow 1
- 9˝ × 12˝ (23 × 30.5cm) sheet of EVA foam
- 8˝ × 10˝ (20.3 × 25.4cm) card stock for folding the template
- Glue stick (recommend acid free)
- Bone folder (recommended)

Additives Required to Prepare Pulp

Yellow Ochre aqueous dispersed pigment

Retention agent

Techniques Needed

Color Recipes, page 54

Make Basic Sheets, page 38

Envelopes, page 66

Using Stencils and Shaped Deckles, page 65

Envelope Templates, page 118

Folding Template, page 119

Preparing the Stencil Deckle

1. Trace the Envelope Templates (page 118) onto a piece of paper.

2. Tape the template onto the sheet of EVA foam, centered.

3. Using a craft knife, cut through the paper and foam on the lines to create the envelope deckle.

4. Remove paper.

5. Trim the edge of the EVA foam to fit the mould as needed. **Ⓐ**

Making the Paper

1. Prepare the vat with Yellow 1 pulp.

2. Using the envelope deckle, pull and couch a card and envelope. **Ⓑ**

3. Continue pulling and couching cards and envelopes until all the pulp is used.

4. Press and dry the papers as usual.

Folding the Card and Envelope

1. Trace the Folding Template (page 119) onto the piece of card stock, and cut it out.

2. Fold the template along the dotted lines.

3. Place the folding template on top of an envelope paper, and align the edges.

4. Fold the flaps of the folding template in, and holding it firmly in place, score around the outside of the template with a bone folder or a butter knife. **Ⓒ**

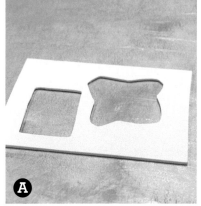
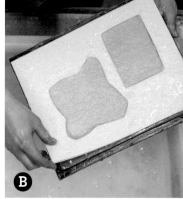
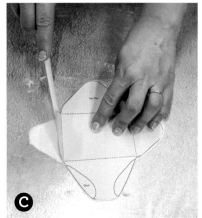

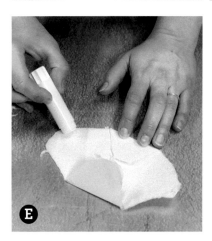

5. Remove the folding template; fold the paper along the scored lines, and run the bone folder along the creases to make them crisp. **Ⓓ**

6. Glue the envelope flaps in place, applying glue to the areas where the flaps overlap. **Ⓔ**

7. Fold the card in half. Use a bone folder to press the crease. **Ⓕ**

8. Insert the card into the envelope.

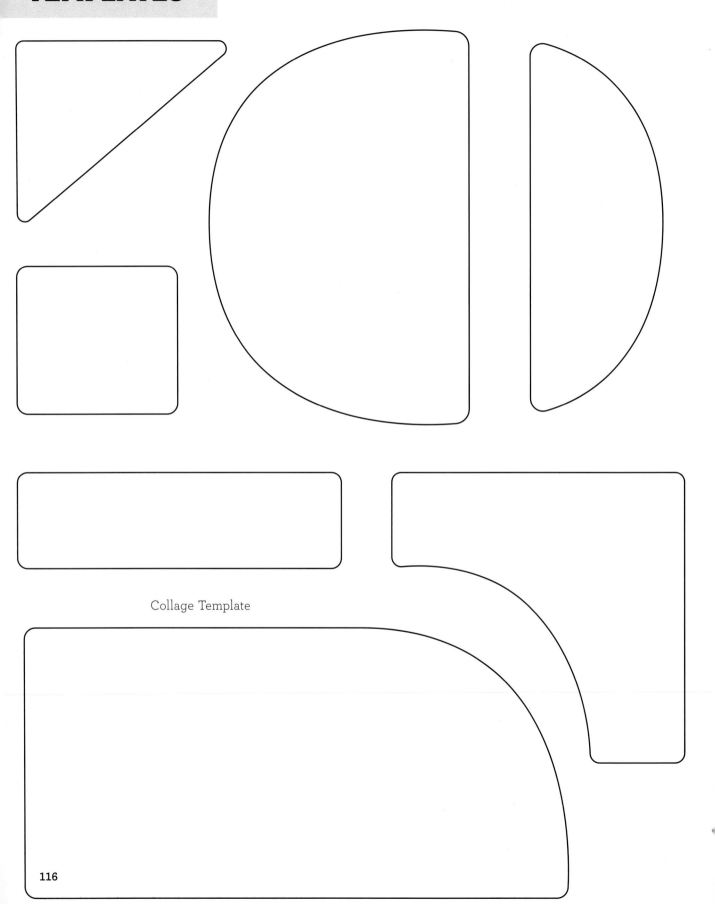

Collage Template

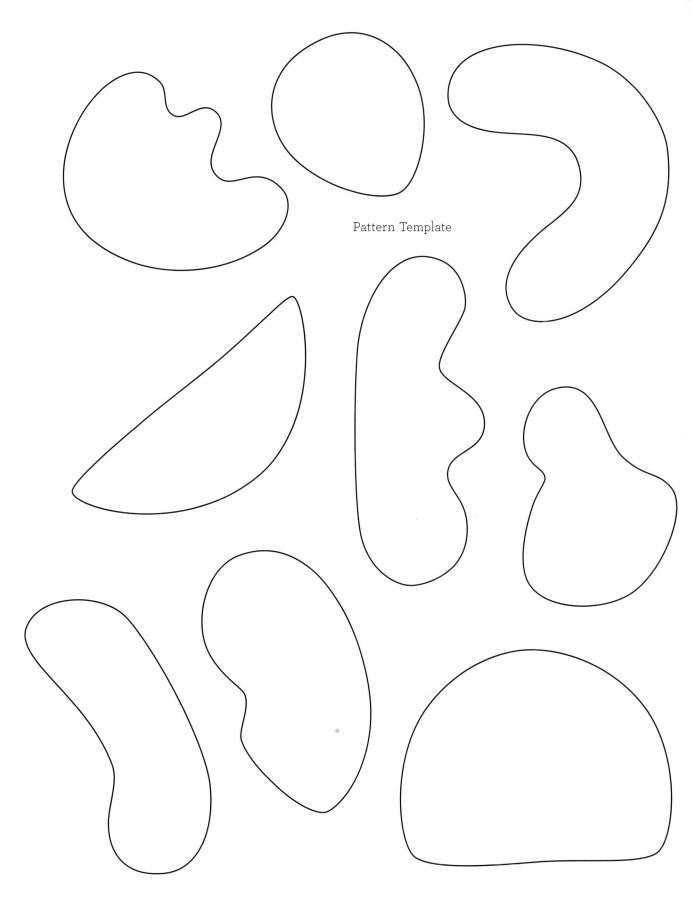

Pattern Template

Envelope Template

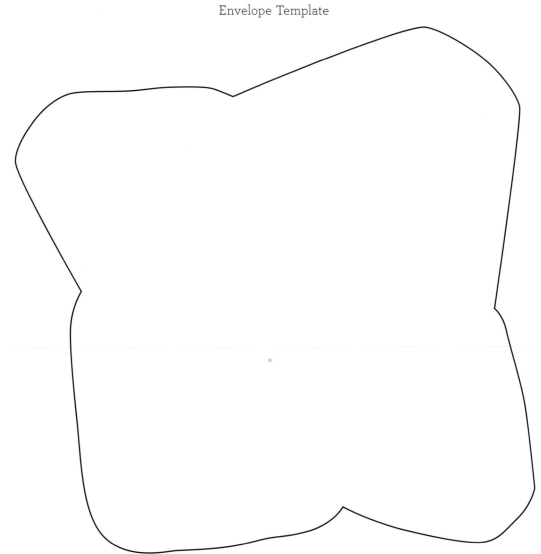

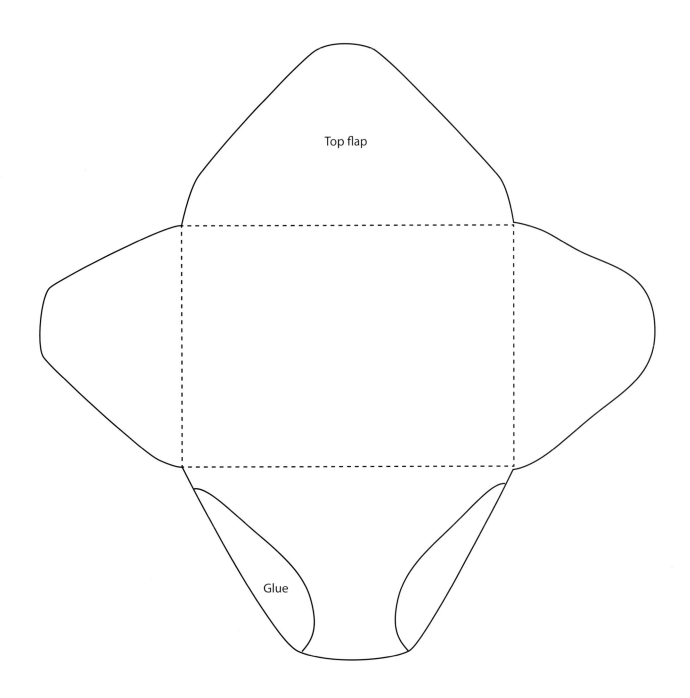

Top flap

Glue

Folding Template

Glossary

Abaca—a plant native to the Philippines, botanical name Musa textilis—leaf-stem fibers are harvested and formed into sheet pulps for use in papermaking

Beating—the process of grinding and macerating fiber into pulp

Calcium Carbonate—or CaCO3, can be added to pulp as alkaline reserve to protect the finished paper from future acids and to make paper more archival and longer lasting

Cellulose—the main component of plant cell walls—any cellulose material can be used to make paper, but the cellulose percentage of plants varies

Cotton—shrub native to tropical regions, botanical name Gossypium—the boll, or fibers around the seed, are almost pure cellulose; cotton materials used for papermaking are by-products of the textile industry

Cotton Linter—short fibers that remain on the cottonseed after first ginning and are then pressed into sheets for papermaking

Cotton Rag—sometimes called comber noil, cotton by-products of the garment industry partially beaten and pressed into sheets for papermaking

Couching—transferring the wet sheet from the mould to a felt— from the French word coucher, meaning "to put to bed" or "to lay down"

Deckle—the empty frame that fits on top of the mould to create the size and shape of the paper—from the German word deckle, meaning "cover" or "lid"

Deckle Edge—the feathery edge on handmade paper, created when pulp seeps under the deckle

Felt—the surface wet sheets are couched onto—traditionally, felted wool blankets were used, but today this term can refer to interfacing sheets used for the same purpose

Fibers—raw, natural materials used for papermaking

Fibril—a fine fragment of fiber created during the beating process—longer beating creates more fibrils in the pulp

Fibrillate—process of raising fibrils on the fiber

Free—describes pulps that drain quickly, usually lighter beaten pulps with fewer fibrils

GSM—also expressed as g/m2, the preferred method for expressing the weight of paper

Kozo—a plant grown in Japan and Thailand, botanical name Broussonetia papyrifera—the highest quality fibers are harvested, bundled, and sold for use in papermaking

Pigment—substance used for coloring pulp

Post—layered stack of wet sheets alternating with felts, built during a papermaking session

Pulp—fibers after they have been beaten or blended into mush

Size/sizing—a material added to paper to reduce its absorbency—sizings can be internal or external (sometimes referred to as surface sizing)

Slurry—mixture of pulp and water at the appropriate ratio to form sheets

Spur—a small grouping of damp sheets of paper that have been pressed and are ready for hang drying

Stuff (pulp stuff)—materials used to make papermaking pulp

Vat—a tub used for paper formation

Index

Resources

Arnold Grummer's—papermaking supplier, especially deckle box moulds
arnoldgrummer.com

Carriage House Paper—papermaking supplier
carriagehousepaper.com

Twinrocker Handmade Paper—papermaking supplier
twinrocker.com

The Papertrail—papermaking supplier in Canada
papertrail.ca

Hand Papermaking—magazine
handpapermaking.org

North American Hand Papermakers
northamericanhandpapermakers.org

International Association of Hand Papermakers and Paper Artists
iapma.info

Robert C. Williams Museum of Papermaking
paper.gatech.edu

University of Iowa's Center for the Book
uicb.uiowa.edu/

Paperslurry—blog by May Babcock, especially map of hand papermakers
paperslurry.com

The Sunday Paper Blog—blog by Helen Hiebert
helenhiebertstudio.com/blog

Bibliography

Asunción, Josep. *The Complete Book of Papermaking*. New York: Lark, 2003.

Baker, Cathleen A. *By His Own Labor*. New Castle, DE: New Castle, 2000.

Baker, Cathleen A. *From the Hand to the Machine*. Ann Arbor, MI: Legacy, 2010.

Barrett, Timothy D. *European Hand Papermaking*. Ann Arbor, MI: Legacy, 2018.

Boyne, Elizabeth. "Making Paper the 'Old Ladies' Way.'" *Hand Papermaking* 33, no. 2 (2018): 3-6.

Dawson, Sophie. *The Art and Craft of Papermaking*. Philadelphia: Running, 1992.

Eyferth, Jacob. *Eating Rice from Bamboo Roots*. Cambridge: Harvard University Press, 2009.

Heller, Jules. *Papermaking*. New York: Watson-Guptil, 1978.

Hiebert, Helen. *The Papermaker's Companion*. North Adams, MA: Storey, 2000.

Hunter, Dard. *Papermaking: History and Technique of an Ancient Craft*. New York: Dover, 1978.

Thomas, Peter, and Donna Thomas. *They Made the Paper at Tuckenhay Mill*. Ann Arbor, MI: Legacy, 2017.

Thomas, Peter, and Donna Thomas. *The Ergonomics of Hand Papermaking*. Youtube, uploaded by Peteranddonna, April 16, 2021, originally produced 1990.

Toal, Bernard. *The Art of Papermaking*. Worcester, MA: David, 1983.

About the Author

Kelsey Pike is a production papermaker based in Kansas City, Missouri. She learned papermaking and started her brand, Sustainable Paper + Craft, while attending the local art institute in 2009. Since then, she has sold more than 200,000 sheets of paper. She specializes in papers specifically designed for artists and makers, made from recycled fabric and other sustainable fibers. Good craft is always Kelsey's priority, so she's continuously studying, practicing, and learning new ways to make the best paper possible. She hopes to pass on her love of this traditional craft through teaching and writing.

Find her online at @Kelseypikepapercraft and sustainablepapercraft.com.

Crafty courses to become an expert maker...

From their studio to yours, Creative Spark instructors are teaching you how to create and become a master of your craft. So not only do you get a look inside their creative space, you also get to be a part of engaging courses that would typically be a one or multi-day workshop from the comfort of your home.

Creative Spark is not your one-size-fits-all online learning experience. We welcome you to be who you are, share, create, and belong.

Scan for a gift from us!

creativespark.ctpub.com